Information at Work

Information at Work
Information management in the workplace

Edited by

**Katriina Byström, Jannica Heinström
and Ian Ruthven**

facet
publishing

Published by Facet Publishing,
7 Ridgmount Street, London WC1E 7AE
www.facetpublishing.co.uk

British Library Cataloguing in Publication Data
A catalogue record for this book is available from the British Library.

ISBN 978–1–78330–275–8 (paperback)
ISBN 978–1–78330–276–5 (hardback)
ISBN 978–1–78330–277–2 (e-book)

First published 2019

Text printed on FSC accredited material.

Cover design by Kathryn Beecroft.
Typeset from editors' files by Flagholme Publishing Services in 11/14 pt Revival 565
and Frutiger
Printed and made in Great Britain by CPI Group (UK) Ltd, Croydon, CR0 4YY.

Contents

List of figures

Acknowledgement

The editors are listed in alphabetical order and have contributed equally to the work (including Chapters 1 and 7).

Contributors

Katriina Byström is Professor of Library and Information Science at Oslo Metropolitan University, Norway and a docent at the University of Borås, Sweden. Her research focuses on information and communication settings at workplaces in general and specifically on work-task based information seeking and retrieval. Dr Byström is an active member of the international academic information science community and a co-founder of the European Network for Workplace Information (ENWI). Her latest research interests target relationships between formulation and performance of work tasks, enactment of information access and everyday workplace learning in digital and hybrid work settings, a research agenda edged by a futuristic notion of '*peopleless offices & officeless people*'. She has authored a number of well-cited publications since 'Task complexity affects information seeking and use' (IPM) in 1995.

Jannica Heinström is Associate Professor of Information Studies at Åbo Akademi University, Finland, and a docent at the University of Borås, Sweden. She received her PhD in Information Studies 2002 from Åbo Akademi University. Dr Heimström's research has been funded by, among others, the Fulbright Association and the Academy of Finland. Her research seeks to understand psychological aspects of information interaction, particularly the role of personality. Her work includes studies on serendipity, information avoidance and inquiry-based learning. Her current project explores individual differences in information sharing attitudes and information literacy in organizations. Dr Heinström has published widely in her field including journal articles, co-edited monographs and the book *From Fear To Flow: Personality and Information Interaction*, Chandos.

Elena Macevičiūtė is Professor of library and information science at the University of Borås, Sweden, and of information and communication sciences at Vilnius University, Lithuania. Her research relates to information use in organizations, digital libraries and resources, and, currently, the role of ebooks and digital reading in modern society. Dr Macevičiūtė has participated in large European research and educational projects and conducted research projects on a national scale in Sweden and Lithuania. She also has participated in development projects in Rwanda, Uganda and Mozambique. She has published over 300 research, educational and professional articles. Dr Macevičiūtė is deputy editor of *Information Research*, an international electronic journal and a member of editorial boards of several other international and national research journals. She has been engaged in the role of expert of higher education study programmes and a research consultant.

Dr Diane Rasmussen Pennington is Lecturer in Information Science and the Course Director for the MSc in Information and Library Studies at the University of Strathclyde. She worked as a corporate information technology professional and then a systems librarian before becoming a full-time academic in 2005. She holds an MS and a PhD in Information Science from the University of North Texas. She is a member of the Strathclyde iSchool Research Group, within which she leads the Information Engagement research area. She is Editor-in-Chief of *Library and Information Research*. Her research seeks to understand and improve how people engage with information, especially online, with an eye toward its role in positive health and well-being. She has published more than 40 works in journals and edited two books: *Social media for academics: A practical guide* and *Indexing and retrieval of non-text information*. Her new book with Facet Publishing, *Social tagging for linked data across environments*, is co-edited with Dr Louise Spiteri.

Nils Pharo is Professor in Knowledge Organization and Information Retrieval at Oslo Metropolitan University, Norway. His research interests are interactive information retrieval, metadata modelling and scholarly communication. Dr Pharo is head of the MetaInfo (Metadata-based information systems) research group. He has written several scientific peer reviewed journal and conference papers.

Ian Ruthven is Professor of Information Seeking and Retrieval at the University of Strathclyde. He has published over 100 articles in the areas of interactive information retrieval and information seeking and edited two collections: *Interactive Information Seeking, Behaviour and Retrieval* (with Diane Kelly) and *Cultural Heritage Information Access and Management* (with Gobinda Chowdhury). He has been programme chair for several major conferences and is on the editorial board of 7 information science journals. He leads one of Europe's largest information science research groups at the Strathclyde ischool. His recent research has included interface design research to help children search for information, information seeking studies on information poverty within marginalised groups and studies on how people use online information to create a sense of happiness.

Jela Steinerová is Professor of Library and Information Science and Head of the Department of LIS, Faculty of Arts, Comenius University in Bratislava, Slovakia. Her main topics of interest are human information behaviour, information science theory and methodology. She has headed several research projects (VEGA, APVV), participated in international projects on digital libraries (DELOS) and information management (ICIMSS) and published monographs and papers. The topics of her research projects include relevance, information ecology, information behaviour in the digital environment. Her monographs focus on information retrieval, information products and creativity, information behaviour and information strategies. She is a member of international editorial and professional boards of conferences (ECIL, CoLIS, ISIC) and journals and editor of the annual review of LIS in the Slovak Republic. She has been a member of the international ENWI expert group project and regularly organizes international conferences *Information Interactions* in Bratislava. Recently she published a monograph on *Information environment and scholarly communication: information ecologies* (2018).

Eric Thivant is Engineer and Associate Researcher in the Magellan Research Centre, at iaelyon Business School, UJML3, University of Lyon, France. He holds also a PhD in Information and Communication Science, obtained in 2003. His research relates to information seeking and use behaviour, especially for professionals, and information management in organizations. He participates in the research projects in semiotics and web semantics in France (Discotec ANR Project), and in international projects such as the ENWI Project (European Network of Workplace Information) with other European research centers (in UK, Germany, Sweden, etc.). He is also a lecturer and teaches courses on website design and database management at iaelyon.

Elaine Toms is Professor of Information Innovation & Management at the Sheffield University Management School, and a member of its Operations Management and Decision Sciences Division. She was formerly Canada Research Chair in Management Informatics, Dalhousie University, Canada, and Associate Professor, University of Toronto, Canada. Her research focuses on two key areas: how technology facilitates (and alternately how it fails) to support human use of information and how to best evaluate when this process meets with success. Within this scope, she has studied browsing in digital newspapers, metaphoric representations in textual menus, the role of genre in information interaction, the effect of task on information access, how interruptions affect the search process, measuring user engagement, how to facilitiate serendipity and how to evaluate search trails. Most recently, she has developed a component-based approach to evaluation. Her research has been supported by a range of organizations including NSERC, SSHRC, CFI, OCLC, EU.

Gunilla Widén is Professor of Information Studies at Åbo Akademi University (ÅAU), Finland and Head of the Library Programme. Her research interests are within two main areas; knowledge management and information behaviour. The aim of the knowledge management research is to understand motives behind information and knowledge sharing using e.g. information culture and social capital theory. The aim of her information behaviour research is to explore how social media affect information behaviour among different groups in society. She has studied e.g. emotions connected to social media use among digital youth and also generational differences in relation to information literacy. She has led several large research projects financed by the Academy of Finland investigating key skills in information society as well as various aspects of social media, changing information behaviour and information literacy. The ongoing Academy of Finland project is on the role of information literacy in the digital workplace (funded 2016-20). She has published widely in her areas of expertise and been appointed expert in several evaluation committees.

Foreword: Situating the role of information in the messy and complex context of the workplace

Annemaree Lloyd

Current trends in workplace research focus on understanding how the nature of work creates the conditions that shape our practice, organize our lives outside work, influence our constructions of identity and create sense of place (Cairns and Malloch, 2011). Definitionally, the term *work* has multiple meanings, referencing a place or an activity which produces something and may or not be remunerated. Various histories have been written about the contribution of work to the transition from agrarian to industrial to post-industrial societies. The concept of paid work has been analysed in relation to power, class, status and gender, divisions of labour and identity, and in the context of practice and performance associated with the operationalisation of work.

Work can therefore be seen as an 'intentional engagement' (Cairns and Malloch, 2011, 7) conducted in places which can more often than not be described as messy and complex. Nowadays, workplaces can be concept-ualised as *fast and shifting* places which are marked by rapid rates of transition and change as organizations compete in markets (commercial and non-commercial) that demand innovation to keep their competitive edge (Lloyd, 2017). The rapid insinuation of technology into all aspects of work complicates any analysis of work, working life or workplaces and has social and economic implications. Technology blurs the traditional boundaries between online and offline work and space, creating new spaces and affording opportunities and imaginings for different kinds of work and different types of working arrangements to emerge, while at the same time introducing threats to employment as organizations downsize and reorganize the nature and the flow of work. While technology creates opportunities for more effective organizational and personal workflow organization and management, it simultaneously creates the potential conditions for risk in relation to data security. In some aspects of work the integration of algorithmic processes as a replacement for human decision making introduces complex questions about transparency, equality and equity.

So how can the workplace be understood from an information science perspective? Where are the starting points for understanding what conditions enable and constrain work, working life and work practices? The thread that weaves through this description of messiness and complexity is that of *information*. Information is the core resource essential to all processes of work and the operationalisation, organization and management of work cannot proceed without it. Access to information enables and constrains our practices and processes. It represents a resource for learning, for managing change, for creating, refining and redeveloping processes and practices and for building our social capitals. Our human need to locate and share information acts as the catalyst for developing social networks and our social and economic labour produces the cultural-discursive, material economic and social-political and historical knowledges that shape our workplaces and the way in which we perform our work, relate to other workers and learn about how work happens (Lloyd, 2010). We advance our competitive edge by sharing information with our working partners and hiding information from our competitors (sometimes from people we work with). We draw not only from explicit information but from socially nuanced information that gives us access to the culture of the workplace, its tacit and unexpressed rules and reflexivities. We also draw from corporeal, physical information which positions us in relation to workplace expertise and the long-term expertise located in embodied information. In effect, information is the catalyst for building workplace resilience in times of rapid and shifting change (Lloyd, 2010; 2013).

It is against this problematisation of work that *Information at Work* emerges, representing a significant and important contribution to guide our understanding of the messiness and complexity of modern workplaces, working life and work practice. *Information at Work* draws from a wide range of theoretical perspectives and epistemological stances, but always situates *information* within the core of the analysis. The authors of this scholarly work have striven to explore and highlight the multiple roles of information in relation to the nature of work, the social and cultural environments in which we work, issues about information management, and identification of the artefacts that enable people to work with information. The recasting of Taylor's (1991) model of the Information Use Environment represents a significant reorientation and highlights the breadth and depth of analysis the authors have undertaken. The expansion of the original model will act as a catalyst for many researchers and demonstrates the significance of an information science perspective to workplace research.

Information at Work represents an important milestone for workplace information research, guiding us through the complexity and messiness of the workplace by showcasing information as the core resource for workplace learning, managing change, developing and implementing organization process, and creating professional networks. I have no doubt that this wonderful book will not only serve the information science field but will become an important resource for other fields where an understanding about the changing nature of work and work practices is of central interest.

References

Cairns, L. and Malloch, M. (2011) Theories of Work, Place and Learning: new directions. In *The Sage Handbook of Workplace Learning*, 3–16.

Lloyd, A. (2010) *Information Literacy Landscapes: information literacy in education, workplace and everyday contexts*, Elsevier.

Lloyd, A. (2013) Building Information Resilient Workers: the critical ground of workplace information literacy. What have we learnt? In *European Conference on Information Literacy*, 22–25 October, Springer, 219–28.

Lloyd, A. (2017) Learning from Within for Beyond: exploring a workplace information literacy design. In Foster, M. (ed.) *Information Literacy in the Workplace*, Facet Publishing, 97–112.

Taylor, R. S. (1991) Information Use Environments. In Dervin, B. (ed.), *Progress in Communication Sciences*, vol. 10, Ablex, Norwood, NJ, 217–55.

1

Work and information in modern society: a changing workplace

Katriina Byström, Jannica Heinström and Ian Ruthven

We live today in a society characterised by quick technological developments and rapid processes of change. Technological developments have automated processes that used to be carried out by manual labour, whilst new professions and work tasks have emerged. Earlier generations were accustomed to lifelong positions in the same company. Nowadays people search for work opportunities in a global market, experience more frequent career changes, must learn new skills throughout their careers and manage the increasingly fluid boundaries between work life and home life. Even our work environments have changed: as Alvin Toffler's (1980) vision of the 'paperless offices' from 50 years ago is now being realised, we are starting to move into the state of 'peopleless offices' in which work is conducted in digital rather than physical spaces. In the peopleless offices, an organization's workforce collectively carry out their work in digital, rather than physical workplaces. Many workplaces are already now hybrids where the work activities addressed, tools utilised and information consumed are the same no matter whether engaged in at the office or at home.

The role of information is essential in all these processes, as a resource for learning, managing change, developing and running processes and creating professional networks. One of the most significant changes in work is the incorporation of information technology into almost every area of work life, changing how we work, where we work and what work we do. This information revolution within our workplaces calls for a new examination of information, information technology and information practices within the modern workplace and this is what this book seeks to do: provide a comprehensive account of information in the modern workplace. It includes a set of chapters examining and reviewing the major concepts within workplace information, from overarching themes of information cultures and information ecologies to strategic concerns of information management and governance, and detailed accounts of the nature of information artefacts themselves. The topic is international and the text reflects this; whilst there are many cultural, geographical and organizational factors that can influence information work environments, there are also strong commonalities that cut across these boundaries.

In this book, we address several aspects of information, as it is used, valued, transformed, captured, viewed, managed, etc., in its relations to formal and informal activities and doings in a workplace. We summarise the study of such phenomena as workplace information. Workplace information relates closely to study of information behaviour and information practice in the context of work. Information behaviour has been defined as 'the totality of human behaviour in relation to sources and channels of information, including both active and passive information seeking, and information use' (Wilson, 2000). It takes the viewpoint of individuals (including e.g. their habits, skills, preferences, psychological factors, as well as affordances of their contexts) in explaining information-related activities. Information practice is used to particularly emphasise social, shared and relational aspects embedded in the context for information-related activities. It takes a collective approach to information and focuses on people as members of various communities and groups, and underlines how social and cultural aspects form continuous and routine ways to deal with information (Savolainen, 2007).

In the remainder of this chapter, we outline some of the broad characteristics of changing workplaces that provoked this text and motivate a new information science perspective on workplace information.

Economic changes and information innovation

The global recession in 2008 created significant challenges across many areas of life. Tighter profit margins have increasingly led companies to downsize and outsource labour. Downsizing processes affect both those who are laid off and need to find a new position in an increasingly competitive environment and those who remain in the organization and often suffer both from the stress of downsizing and an increased workload

(Dragano, Verde and Siegrist, 2005). Reduced government revenues have led to reduced funding for public-sector organizations that need to absorb cuts whilst demonstrating greater accountability for their funding. This often leads to calls for greater use of information management, better decision-making processes and new information working practices to reduce staff costs. In this context the importance of flexibility, adjustment, developing new skills and information transfer between remaining employees in an organization and the ones leaving, is crucial. Information management processes also become essential in handling the change process as well as the development of the institution (Hayes, 2018).

As a consequence of the need to rationalise, attention has focused on how technology innovations can reduce costs. This means that many work tasks and professions may disappear in the coming few decades. Drastically, Frey and Osborne (2013) found that nearly 47% of work as we know it today may be handled by computerised systems in the USA in the next two decades, and a recent report in Sweden arrived at the conclusion that 53% of today's work can disappear in the same time period (Fölster and Hultman, 2014). This forces a lot of attention on how and what to automate and a new stream of work-related information innovation research.

These rapid processes of change in organizations have become even more frequent, which tests workers' ability to adapt and adjust. Reorganization of work tasks and workflows is a recurrent change process. New technology, such as social media tools, bring with them demands for learning (Sloan and Quan-Haase, 2017). Presence on social media is today a must for many organizations but often with little solid evidence on what strategies work and which do not. Responsibility for decision making is also becoming increasingly decentralised and moving employees closer to customers (Ouye, 2011). This change has led to a higher independence and responsibility for the individual employee, including responsibility for managing personal learning processes, allocation of time and focusing of attention (O'Leary, Mortensen and Woolley, 2011). As personal responsibility increases, personal information management is also becoming increasingly important, since swift access to relevant information often depends on structuring and managing information relevant to various work tasks. Sustainability has increased in importance, with implications, for instance, for costs of office space, which is an argument for telecommuting. Workers are also demanding more flexibility to where and when they work (Ouye,

2011), which places attention on how to support information access and use in mixed environments.

Information technology and its impact on people

Digital technology has had a major impact on work processes, and increasingly so due to developments of mobile technology in recent years. The current work ecology consists of an environment with a wide variety of different modes and devices for communication technology (Wajcman and Rose, 2011). This offers flexibility but also comes with an increased demand for connectivity and availability. With mobile technology, people get used to instant and constant access to information. This influences their own workflows, such as quickly looking up facts and practical information as an integrated part of the work process. The drawback of communication and information technologies is the often-reported stress of the constant pressure to be available (Barley, Meyerson and Grodal, 2011). The constant access to technology comes with an expectation to be reachable 24/7.

Access to technology 24/7 blurs the division between work and leisure, which can have both positive and negative effects. The ability to work anytime and anywhere invites work to invade times and places that used to be devoted to leisure and family (Murray and Rostis, 2007). This in turn can make it more difficult to disengage from work, which in turn creates stress (Boswell and Olson-Buchanan, 2007). The increasing pace and volume of work as well as the challenges of balancing work with family and leisure have long been cited as a source of stress for many workers (Jacobs and Gerson, 2001) and the introduction of the internet has given rise to whole new areas of academic study on work behaviour (Hertel, Johnson and Passmore, 2017).

The constantly growing flow of e-mail and other communication modes has been cited as a source of stress for many information workers (Boswell and Olson-Buchanan, 2007). New research, however, states that the notion of e-mail causing stress is not a matter of the number of e-mails, but rather a part of the general overload and feeling of being overwhelmed that is caused by daily communication activities that are beyond the worker's control. Working across time zones also extends the work day, as messages might appear from colleagues all over the world. In other words, the actual stressor may be a workforce dominated by downsizing and globalisation rather than communication technology (Barley et al., 2011). Identifying what information management approaches enhance work practices and which cause problems is non-trivial but essential for good information work practices.

Fragmentation

Constant connectivity is currently changing the very nature of knowledge work. Common workdays consist of short work episodes which involve a variety of mediated communication. The access to social media and other communication technologies have made work processes more fragmented, as presence on social media is accessible and sometimes expected at all times. Work tasks have also become more fragmented. Workers spend less time at each work task and switch tasks frequently. Studies have found that more than half of work spheres are interrupted during a typical workday (Mark, Gudith and Klocke, 2008). Flexibility and multitasking are all the more required at the workplace.

New information technology also causes frequent interruptions to the workflow. It has been estimated that a third of e-mails request action, in other words signify a new work task (Dabbish et al., 2005, 696, cited in Barley, Meyerson and Grodal, 2011). This also means that the flow of e-mail creates work additional to that which perhaps was planned for the day. Studies have found that information workers on average are interrupted every 12 minutes (Mark, Gudith and Klocke, 2005). Half of the time, this interruption comes from workers themselves, switching from one task to another (Jin and Dabbish, 2009). An alternative view to the notion of some work tasks 'interrupting' others, the constant flow of multiple unconnected tasks is managed by the workers themselves and a natural part of today's knowledge work (Wajcman and Rose, 2011). Classical notions of information tasks therefore may need to be reinterpreted into ones that fit with modern ways of working to allow us to theorise more usefully about work tasks and promote good ways of conducting these tasks.

Information technology and its impact on organizations

Rapid changes to information infrastructures are changing the nature of work, forcing a reinvention of old practices and the creation of new ones. For example, bloggers and online newspapers are now as influential as traditional journalism; social media are now a key means of interacting with customers instead of direct marketing; many services such as banking, buying a home, booking travel and commerce are now primarily online activities created by experts in digital environments rather than experts in built environments; government services are increasingly online services; and so on. The vast amount of internet information means that even traditional information experts such as doctors are taking on larger roles in explaining information rather than providing information. There is hardly a discipline or area of work that is not touched by new technology.

The relatively inexpensive information storage available now means organizations can capture massive amounts of data that can be mined to provide more robust decision making about managing cities, predicting demographic changes, tailoring marketing campaigns or managing simple performance. How this information is stored, organized, classified, shared and secured are classic information management concerns which need new proven solutions. Many organizations are moving towards cloud services, forcing hard discussions about which information to store, where it is stored and who has access rights to this information. The valuable nature of much of this information and our reliance on it raises new security threats: how can we protect our data if we don't have physical storage of it, how can we safely share data and how do we help employees understand information security risks?

This change in how we store, manage and make available information is set against a fluid background of changing legislation surrounding what organizations can and cannot do with information. Rights to access information, rights to information privacy, rights to data protection and other assorted information laws vary locally, nationally and internationally, resulting in a complex and shifting network of laws, policies and guidelines that institutions must create systems and practices to manage.

Global trends

Most attention has been devoted to information work in developed, Westernised countries. The digital divide does exist and impacts on work information. Workers in some countries struggle to obtain what seems basic in other countries, such as electricity supply to obtain internet access. Whilst the internet has opened up access to global information, the majority of this information is in a relatively small number of languages, and most internet tools still work best for these majority languages. The situation is changing, however, with areas such as the Middle East and Latin America making major strides in providing information infrastructure and global giants such as Google being heavily challenged by regional alternatives such as Yandex and Baidu.

What happens in more affluent countries often serves as models for new information services and practices in developing countries. This is particularly the case for services such as e-government or customer services, where younger, more affluent and more digitally connected people are requesting new types of interaction with companies and government (Deng, Karunasena and Xu, 2018). How to provide these new services is not yet clear, as successful Western models may not translate into other cultures with different practices, social norms and experiences of digital services.

These are trends. Not every trend affects every worker or organization in the same way but the general trend is towards more reactive processes, faster methods of interacting with information and information users, and more complex information environments followed by new practices, management policies and legislation. All these trends and their impact on individuals and organizations force new attention on our information in our workplaces.

Work information environments

Workplaces are commonly conceptualised as physical places where people are situated to engage in work activities. This broad identification of work 'place' with a physical location is still most people's understanding of their workplace, as being the place in which they carry out work. The range of workplaces in which we can engage in work is vast, spanning from spaces that are reassigned as workspaces (such as bedrooms transformed into home offices), spaces which become workplaces even though not designed as such (emergency services attending a roadside accident or surveyors, builders, and architects meeting at a development site) to spaces that are that are purposively constructed to centralise work (factories, markets, hospitals, universities, etc.). An individual's work may be entirely within one workplace setting or require movement between workplace settings, such as a family doctor visiting patients or a lawyer moving between office, court and prison.

The stereotypical office setting is a common experience for many of us and those of us who have an office will probably think of this space when we are asked to imagine 'where we work'. But where we actually conduct our work may vary across many places depending on the tasks in which we are engaged. Our information use *environments*, therefore, are not simply a matter of place but of the various places in which we conduct our information work, how we decide (or have decided for us) what work happens where and what information technology is present or available within those spaces. The design of 'material' office environments is increasingly recognised as an important tool for work processes, as working spaces are planned according to work processes rather than work tasks. For instance, the provision of spaces for serendipitous meetings and team work is gaining ground. The importance of space for innovation and creativity has been underlined.

Recently, information technology has broadened the notion of work 'place' in two ways. First, communication technology has allowed the creation of digital workplaces in which we work with other people who are not co-located in the same physical environment. This can result in the closest work colleagues being physically distant. Second, technology such as smartphones and tablets has allowed us to carry out work activities in locations that were not previously seen as work locations, such as writing documents on the train or checking e-mail in restaurants. Whether such flexibility is a good thing is still a matter of much debate, but certainly the move towards on-demand access to work information, at least in technology-heavy Western workplaces, has created new choices about how we work and when we work.

This broadening of the place of work also forces new attention on how information supports, or doesn't support, so much technology-mediated information work. How do we store, access, share or simply manage work that moves beyond the office walls and is not contained within traditional work environments? Some of these decisions are made for us by institutional or government decision-making bodies that mandate use of certain technology, some arise from consensus amongst teams who decide on the approach that works best for an individual situation, and others may simply arise from individual convenience, customs and preferences.

The nature of the information systems being used can be well aligned or poorly aligned to the information work actually being done and can be good for some users and poor for others. There are many axes we could draw here that differentiate types of information-use environments. There is a risk of drawing straw men and oversimplifying information-use environments but some distinctions at least point to how much variation there is within information-work environments.

- How many systems are used? Some work roles may require regular, dedicated use of one or two systems (workers in a call centre for example), whereas other roles may require use of many systems with few apparent guidelines, beyond experience, on how to choose between them. Forensic investigators or patent lawyers, two closely related fields, have to navigate different systems to gather pieces of information, often only guided by hunches, to assemble enough evidence to solve a problem.
- How formally defined are procedures for conducting work tasks? Some work tasks are formally codified in processes that are part of company procedure or legally defined processes (rules for presenting information in court, for example), whereas other work tasks (such as writing this document) are ones created on the fly by individual actors, and only the output is assessed.
- What is the nature of the work being undertaken? Some work environments, such as health environments, are heavily regulated with a high degree of compliance to standards, legislation and public accountability. Others, such as journalism, are also information-heavy, but where direct legislation is usually far lighter and information gives a competitive edge, sources are often deliberately hidden and success has a quantifiable market-led measure.
- How is information on work organized and made available? Information on how work is to be done can be part of clearly defined criteria and processes available to all in the institution or it can be a nebulous understanding that arises through the conduct of work itself. Often work is a mixture of both; nurses have clearly defined processes for examining patients and recording patient data, whereas understanding how to calm a confused and anxious patient comes from experience. Some work tasks have commonly agreed standards between institutions on how the task is to be performed and knowledge of these tasks can aid movement between institutions; many other tasks are based on locally defined 'how we do this here' approaches.

• How reliant is work success on the individuals conducting the work and how reliant is it on good information processes? In some fields instinct, experience and domain knowledge are important personal attributes contributing to success. Lawyers, for example, all have access to the same legal information but some are better at using this information than others. In other fields, such as software engineering, the ideal situation, expressed through measures such as the Capability Maturity Model (Doss et al., 2017), rates processes that are less dependent on individuals and more dependent on good management as being better processes. So how do work environments develop in such different ways, and how can good information practices overcome widely differing skill levels in workers? Part of the answer to the last question is in acknowledging that workplaces themselves are also social spaces and spaces where we spend much of our time, if we are lucky enough to be in work.

Information use environments are thus highly contextual phenomena. The diversity and complexity of workplace information makes it extremely challenging to unpick what makes good information use environments, but even being able to identify key generalities within such diverse settings could lead to power guidelines for information management. It also raises questions on how to investigate such issues, which are tackled in the next section.

Perspectives on workplace information

Work is a core area of human existence and many researchers have undertaken workplace information studies. Within the literature there are many different approaches in which we can, and have, researched on workplace information, including focusing on individuals, teams, groups, projects and social (work) practices, both at a local and general level – systems, processes and organizations. There is no right perspective or correct unit of analysis; rather there are many approaches even when studying the same concept which can yield complementary insights into workplace information.

Workplace information may be approached, for example, from an organizational/managerial level (as often within information management), divided into different systems and 'owned' by different departments. Sometimes the same information is stored and displayed by different systems that can cause problems when they are not updated simultaneously. In this light, workplace information becomes an object of categorisations and contents in databases and personal files. Information is a resource to be cultivated, organized and harvested through different systems. This kind of information is readily studied with a system orientation that is based in linearly logical relationships in organizational processes and hierarchies. Within organizations, information culture significantly influences information work (Widén-Wulff, 2005, 32) such as information sharing and collaboration (Hansen and Widén, 2017).

Workplace information has also a social side; that is, different groupings within the workplace may interact differently with the same information and may value it differently, depending on shared traditions and tacitly understood agreements. This information is often positively related to the goals and visions of the group, and since goals and visions of different actors may vary more or less, thus the value placed on information may also vary. In order to be goals and visions that guide the activities in the workplace, they need to be shared to a certain degree. In order to reach this, the groups need to have developed a way of relating to each other in the workplace. Most workplaces have throughout their history developed activities, ways of behaviour and a number of information sources that are based on beliefs of what information is needed, useful and valuable in different work activities. This kind of view of information is bound into practices that structure the work activities themselves, what is expected to be done and in what manner. Whereas part of such practices are global (like the duties of a dentist in general), the local variations may be huge (a dentist fixing a root filling in a high-tech clinic in Manhattan compared with a dentist attending to the 'same' tooth in a small health centre in a rural area of a developing country).

A major change in the organization of work processes over the last 50 years has been a shift from hierarchical structures towards more emphasis on team work, at times in multi-team organizations (Marks et al., 2005). An increased use of telecommunication tools allow synchronous and asynchronous communication, which increases opportunities to build teams across nations. For instance, wikis or cloud services offer ample ground for communication, information sharing, collaborative information processes and co-creating of information, as do teleconferencing platforms. The composition of teams is often fluctuating and employees are frequently members of several teams, e.g. by wikis or other collaborative tools online.

Saying that work is social does not of course mean democratic or equal; class distinctions can be, to a degree, created or removed through the way physical spaces are arranged and how workers are arranged within those spaces. The social is important, however, in much of the interaction that surrounds work; the interaction that helps pass on knowledge from one generation to the next, the interaction that creates shared understandings of how to conduct difficult tasks, the interaction that makes sense of what the organization is trying to achieve, the interaction that stratifies people into roles and encourages information hiding, the interaction that fails to understand each other that can lead to disenfranchised workers and the interaction that encourages co-operation or collaboration.

From a sociological perspective, larger societal processes such as generational differences may influence how workers act in the workplace. New generations are entering the workplace with their own expertise and demands. Baby boomers (born 1944–64) have been found to be accustomed to hierarchies and resistant to change and new technology (Parry and Urwin, 2011). Generation Y (born 1980–2000) again are generally technology oriented, connected 24/7 and are skilful at multi-tasking (Haynes, 2011). Dealing with new technological developments and the information overload it often creates has also shown an age difference in experiences. Older people (61–70 years) experience lack of skill in using technology as a factor, reducing their work efficiency and productivity, and 51–60-year-olds particularly find the work/leisure balance challenging (Benselin and Ragsdell, 2015).

Workplace information is also related to the individual worker. Depending on the individual's motivation, beliefs, goals and visions, workplace information gets an additional dimension. The experiences and knowledge that any worker needs and gains while attending work duties in the workplace cannot simply be reduced to the workplace practices, even though they are naturally related. Individuals use and organize information out of their understanding of their duties, as well as their own ideas about where they are going. Moreover, the practices are dependable on the individuals, since all workplace information does not fit into – formal or informal – systematised information structures. Part of this knowledge is tacit, which by definition it is not possible to make completely explicit; part of it is explicit but for different reasons not adapted to formal information systems. One reason may be that the individual perceives the information as informal or of extreme (un)ordinariness. This also makes the knowledge that the individual possesses highly difficult to 'manage'. Individual differences from a psychological perspective have been found to influence work ethic, commitment to the workplace, openness to change processes and adaptability and coping in processes of change (Arshad and Sparrow, 2010; Stark, Thomas and Poppler, 2000; Brennan and Skarlicki, 2004).

Expertise, skill and experience are other evident influential factors in workers' ability to perform their tasks. The work role of professionals also influences their information behaviour (Leckie, Pettigrew and Sylvain, 1996) Different professions come with not only differences in work task and skills, but also norms, values and professional cognitive authority (Wilson, 1983). This influences information processes within the profession (Sundin and Hedman, 2005). Most studies on work roles and professions have focused on knowledge workers. Emerging research shows that mobile and physical work processes may underlie other information processes. The role of intuition for the work of policemen has been underlined (Allen, 2011) as well as the role of experiential and embodied information of ambulance workers (Lloyd, 2009).

Finally, models of information ecology place the individual's information processes within a broader context (Huvila, 2011; Widén, Steinerová and Voisey, 2014) and this has given rise to a series of models of workplace information behaviour which we present in the next section.

Models of workplace information[1]

Models depicting information acquisition and use at work have a long history in information behaviour research and form a solid basis for today's research on workplace information (Byström, Ruthven and Heinström, 2017). In the late 1960s there were two *Annual Review of Information Science and Technology (ARIST)* reviews on 'information needs and uses' that illustrated the ways in which professionals, at this period often engineers and scientists, acquired information in their work. In the review by Paisley (1968), the analysis resulted in an illustration of a scientist within a layer of systems. The systems were embedded in each other and the information needs and information-seeking activities by scientists were expected to relate to them. The information-related activities were linked to the characteristics of the scientist and the world she interacted with in work issues. Paisley describes this set of systems as 'almost-concentric'.

The outer system is the cultural frame of the society. It is pervasive on the values and the overall aims of information acquisition, and probably the most difficult to resist aligning to, since the 'success' is defined in terms of society-wide acknowledged measures. The next three systems with increasingly more alternatives for an individual scientist are (ideological) political system(s), (professional/disciplinary) membership group(s) and (interest-based) reference group(s).

The next subset of systems is expected to have an increasingly more active role in the scientist's information acquisition. The first system is the invisible college of peers who keep contact and share information directly among each other. The 'invisible college' was reinvented by De Solla Price and Beaver (1966) in the 1960s and referred originally to a closed society of the most influential scientists within a given field in the 17th century. In the De Solla Price revision, all researchers create their own invisible college, a network based on the social ties among the members. Rather than just being a loose network, the conception comes closer to communities of practice (CoP), a conception coined later on by Lave and Wenger (1991). Whereas the invisible college is a group of people with similar status and often similar views but dispersed geographically, the system of formal organization refers to the organization of people brought together by a workplace within which certain information channels and sources are provided. A subsystem within the workplace is the scientist's own work team, which consists of people she interacts with on a daily basis and together with whom she acquires and uses information. Paisley places the scientist herself in the middle of all these social systems and refers to individual characteristics such as cognitive structure, intelligence, creativity and motivation that modify her perception of information. Right across these 'almost-concentric' systems there are legal/economic systems as well as formal information systems. The latter one includes information centres such as libraries, mass media and educational institutions that mediate information in the society at large.

In a later text, Paisley (1980, 136) states that social systems frame work by mandating, justifying, enabling, guiding, evaluating and rewarding it. The framing may take different forms; for instance, the formal organization enables work by providing space, equipment and material for work activities, whereas the work team enables it by providing knowledge and support. Paisley identifies the trinity of properties of information, characteristics of the individual and constructions of social context that has become increasingly important in modern information studies. He also points to the evolution of work as an important converging factor for information acquisition and use at work. Returning to the 1968 text by Paisley, the quality of research on information acquisition depends on how well the research considers aspects such as the full array of available information sources, the intended use of information, the personal characteristics of the worker, e.g. professional orientation and motivation, the social, political and economic context and the consequences that information has when put into use (Paisley, 1968, 2).

Only a year later, Allen (1969) published another major review in which some material overlapped with Paisley's review. However, most of the 58 referenced articles originated from 1968 or 1969, which demonstrates a high research interest on information acquisition and use in work at the end of the 1960s. Allen, building on Paisley's review, views an individual (engineer or scientist) as an information processor who interacts in her research group, in her organization, in her professional society, in her invisible college and within the formal information system. Allen concludes that research on information acquisition and use is carried out from cognitive psychology, organizational psychology and sociology, a needed combination since 'virtually nothing is known . . . [on] communications in organizations' in the late 1960s, 'yet communications is the keystone of organizational functioning' (Allen, 1969, 24). In their empirical work, Allen and his colleagues found ways of working by 'gatekeepers' to share information in their informal networks (e.g. Allen and Cohen, 1969), that colleagues were the best information source for much information at workplaces (e.g. Allen, 1969) as well as that information sources requiring least effort were the ones most often chosen for use (Gerstberger and Allen, 1968). Many of these findings have been studied and found to hold even in later research at workplaces, and remain as important phenomena in the study of digital workplaces.

Salancik and Pfeffer (1978) introduced a social information processing approach in which they redefined the main concepts of Need–Satisfaction models: 'needs', 'wants' and 'desires'. These terms invoke a variety of positions that would address the current criticism of the usage of 'information-need' in information studies. In Salancik and Pfeffer's approach, the social context in which the individual is engaged provides socially acceptable beliefs, attitudes and needs, as well as reasons for action; and it also highlights certain information, together with a set of expectations and consequences. Salancik and Pfeffer provide an insightful framework of the social nature of work and the social and personal construction of that reality where 'people learn what their needs, values, and requirements should be in part of their interactions with others' (1978, 230). A central dimension of the social construction is the ways in which (new) employees rely on their colleagues for information about the salient aspects of work, as well as about appropriate norms, standards, attitudes and needs at the workplace. As for individual choices in constructing an understanding of work as social phenomena, Salancik and Pfeffer put forth two aspects. 'Commitment' tends to make people loyal to – and in due time uncritical of – views and attitudes related to the committed work situation. 'Rationalised action' relates to commitment in the sense that people once committed tend to develop justifications for their decisions and ways of behaving that make these meaningful and explicable. Both of these aspects are important for understanding information acquisition and use at work.

Salancik and Pfeffer's framework indicates that we indeed may learn the most about individual behaviour at work by studying the informational and social setting of a workplace. Another framework with an organization-theoretical orientation was offered by Daft and Lengel, whose take on information acquisition was concerned with the kinds of information mediated and the characters of channels for mediation. They work from the assumption that work organizations are 'open social systems that must process information . . . to accomplish internal tasks, to coordinate diverse activities, and to interpret the external environment' (Daft and Lengel, 1986, 555). They proposed that unanalysable, equivocal issues are best solved by 'rich' media, which allow a swift and varied way to interpret views. Characteristic for rich media is the simultaneous presentation of several informational cues, instant feedback, personal focus and natural language use (face-to-face meeting being a highly rich medium, a 'lean' medium such as e-mail less so). From an organizational point of view, the choices between channels and sources for information are part of organizational efficiency. Later on, in the same line of reasoning, Choo (2006) placed a heavy emphasis on organizational culture and presents structures that provide different prerequisites for information acquisition and use in organizations. During a process mode, information acquisition and use is intensive and well organized, where specific and well informed decision making is a central goal. In political mode, information acquisition and use is directed by an aim to support preferred decisions; both intensity and control are relatively high but biased. In rational mode, the intensity and control over information acquisition and use in decisions is rather low, and guided by principle of 'good enough'. Finally, in anarchy mode, the intensity and control over information acquisition and use in decisions is low, best described as *ad hoc* and random. The frameworks above indicate a view of the acquisition and use of information as phenomena that characterise and affect our understanding of work itself, rather than a neutral consequence of a neutral need for information as a part of work activity. Wersig and Windel (1985) were among the first to declare that sources and channels of information are part of information actions, and that these may undertake agency and thus assume a role of actors themselves.

Wilson and Walsh's (1996) model of information behaviour underlines the person in a context. An information need activates information-seeking behaviour, which can be in the form of passive attention, passive search, active search or ongoing search. There are, however, intervening variables that interfere with the process. They may be psychological, demographic, role-related, interpersonal, environmental or related to the information sources. Information behaviour is, moreover, a cyclic process, where information processing and use may lead to new information needs. The model is relevant also in a work context, as it not only describes the interaction between the employee and the work context as forming information behaviour, but also underlines the complex process that follows an information need. In a work context there are continuously several barriers as well as enablers to meet an information need. Individual employees' personal ways of handling information, such as habits of personal information management, interact with work-related enablers and constraints (such as suggested information systems for information management).

Yet another alternative to approaching information acquisition and use at workplaces has taken work tasks as a central starting point, contrasting the general approaches on work and work roles. Rasmussen, Pejtersen and Goodstein (1994, 25, 206) place tasks as an analytical level between levels of individual and work domain; an individual worker (actor) is placed at the centre of their work analysis framework, which highlights the actor's competency, criteria and values. The work analysis may then take place on cognitive, activity and domain levels in order to design and evaluate information systems tailored for a specific workplace. Closest to an individual is the layer of cognitive resources available and required. The next three layers focus on analysing the activity engaged in: how can the task situation be defined in terms of mental strategies available for use, in decision-making terms and in terms of work domain? The last analytical layer addresses specifically the work domain in terms of means–ends structure by which the desired goal is imagined and then strategies to achieve it are determined.

Byström and Järvelin (1995) introduced a work task-based framework that focused on what type of information was needed for work tasks of varying complexity and from what channels and sources this information was retrieved. The framework has further been developed by Byström and Hansen (2005) as well as Ingwersen and Järvelin (2005). Of the later frameworks, Byström and Hansen (2005, cf. Byström, 1999) focuses specifically on information-related activities at workplaces. The acquisition and use of information from one source is seen in relation to information from other sources with a joint aim to accomplish the work task at hand. The acquisition and use of information happens as part of task performance, from initiation to completion of a work task, indicating a dynamic development of and between perceived task requirements and information acquisition and use. Ingwersen and Järvelin (2005) take a more generic approach and focus specifically on the use of information systems and information searching for (work) tasks or other interests that a person may have. Both frameworks see information acquisition and use as a part of an activity larger than the interaction with a single information source or system. Whereas Ingwersen and Järvelin emphasise the cognitive perspective, Byström and Hansen are more concerned with performing work in actual work situations. Later on, Byström and Lloyd (2012) investigated conceptions of work tasks and the related information acquisition and use through a practice theoretical lens, concluding that information acquisition and use in work tasks illuminate work practices in general and information practices in particular.

The frameworks for information acquisition and information use for work have traditionally focused on goal-directed utilisation of information (inter)mediated in or by documents or people. After a few, but sporadic, exceptions of sources relying on observation through senses (e.g. Byström, 1996, on journalists visiting places and events as source of information; Gorman, 1995, on medical doctors acquiring information by examining patients; McKenzie, 2004, on information practices of midwives; Veinot, 2007, on a vault inspector using bodily senses to acquire information for work), Lloyd (2010) finally introduces a framework of information landscapes of work. Information landscapes consist of textual, social and corporeal information in workplaces, and she argues that all three are important in workplace learning for professionals, especially within professions that traditionally have been not viewed as knowledge workers. Blue-collar professionals depend not only on knowledge based on written or spoken language, but to a considerable degree on bodily mediated formation. During the past decade or so, workplace learning and workplace information practices have become phenomena of increasing importance for understanding information acquisition and use at work. As part of participation in workplace activities, employees grow into their professional roles and learn the implicit and explicit regulations, norms and structures, including the legitimised ways of acquiring and using information (cf. Lave and Wenger, 1991).

Together, the above approaches illustrate that information acquisition and use are dependent on individual choices, but not independent of the social norms and structures (cf. Giddens, 1984). Towards the end of the 1990s, there were two broad traditions that conveyed information systems and information-related activities from 'hard' and 'soft' perspectives in information science. According to Checkland and Holwell (1998), the former is a legacy of Herbert Simon's influential work in organizational studies, with a heavy emphasis on decision making as rational problem solving, and the latter owes a great deal to Sir Geoffrey Vickers' work. Vickers' theory on appreciative systems explains organizational life as based on a process of relationship maintenance in which historically and contextually bound interactions influence the judgements of possible courses of action. For information and information sources, these perspectives offer different conceptualisations either as an aid to reach a specific goal or as part of interpreting and organizing the situation, indeed to understand a world. As the focus is shifted from an objective judgement to situated sense-making, the notions of 'rational' action and 'relevant' information themselves become relative. The skirmish of 'hard' and 'soft' perspectives that dates back to the 1970s has no doubt fed the theoretical development of the field of information science, with the views of today stretching between polarised ones at both ends and a number of more moderate approaches to understand diverse aspects of information-related activities at work.

In the following we present Taylor's model of 'information use environments' (IUE) in more detail, as this model has particularly influenced our work.

Taylor's information use environments

In 1991, Taylor coined 'information use environments' as contextual phenomena that explained differences of information acquisition and use by different professionals on a general level. He claims that differences in information acquisition and use are a result of a number of characteristics of people involved, problems, settings, problem resolutions, perceptions of information and decision processes. Legislators' work is fundamentally different from medical doctors' work, which explains formations of their IUE. Some years later, Leckie, Pettigrew and Sylvain (1996) proposed a framework for information acquisition and use, emphasising the work roles and their associated tasks. Based on a review of studies focusing on professionals' information acquisition and use at work, they conclude that within any profession several sub-roles emerge to a varying degree: information is sought and used in the roles and tasks of a service provider, an administrator/manager, a researcher, an educator and a student. The general frameworks for work demonstrate that different professions come with differences not only in roles, task and skills, but also in norms, values and professional cognitive authority. Alongside the developments in practical work and the values and norms connected to it, professions create their own standards and practices for information-related activities (cf. Taylor, 1991).

In his seminal paper from the early 1990s, Taylor (1991) points out that studies of information at workplaces were predominantly approached from the perspective of either technology or content. Nearly three decades later, we can conclude that the technological approach especially has kept its strong footing as a main signifier of information for most work organizations. It is still the technological advancements that are central in describing

> . . . the size, shape, function, dynamism, and even the content of information systems. That is to say, what is and can be stored in a book (report, paper, or other formal retrievable message) or in a computer memory defines what is accepted as knowledge or information. (Taylor, 1991, 218)

Similarly, the content-driven approach, where the way to organize information/knowledge overrides the information/knowledge itself, and 'locks' it in the constructed structures, has endured. As a result, many workplaces suffer from legacy systems that rely on both old technology and old structures. To mitigate such negative effects, Taylor suggested the information uses-driven approach that

> looks at *the user and the uses of information*, and the contexts within which those users make choices about what information is useful to them at particular times. These choices are based, not only on subject matter, but on other elements of the context within which a user lives and works.
>
> (Taylor, 1991, 218; italics in original)

This approach fits well with the focus on practices winning ground, especially in social sciences, in the 21st century.

We sympathise with Taylor's view and find it very relevant to modern workplaces. In order to enhance the information uses-driven approach, Taylor put forward a tentative model of IUE that has got some, but still surprisingly little, attention in research on workplace information. Below, we introduce the model and make an effort to update it for the field of research on workplace information.

For Taylor, a key feature of information was its usefulness, not as a static characteristic of information, but as a situation-sensitive quality that is only determinable by the person in the situation. Despite this seemingly individual-oriented delineation, Taylor was solely interested in groups of people and their mutual understandings of 'usefulness' in the situations where they

> acted as active, experienced, and critical users of information. That is to say, that they are aware of their problems; they know, at least in approximate terms, where they can find useful information; and they have a critical sensitivity to what constitutes a solution, or, better said, resolution of a problem in their context.
>
> (Taylor, 1991, 219)

The heavy emphasis on usefulness in work settings is also reflected by his choice to only focus on formal information, 'which is sought in the context of recognised problems or concerns', and which 'responds, and is perceived as – and is intended to be – relevant to a particular problem' (Taylor, 1991,

220). Such information may be in formats both oral and recorded, as well as verbal and non-verbal. In addition, information may be used in form of 'raw information or *symptoms*' or as 'interpreted information or *signs*' (Taylor, 1991, 249).

Taylor described an IUE as a work context consisting of

> the set of those elements that (a) affect the flow and use of information messages into, within, and out of any definable entity; and (b) determine the criteria by which the value of information messages will be judged.
>
> (Taylor, 1986, 25–6, 218)

More precisely, he identified 'sets of people, typical structure and thrust of problems of those sets of people, typical settings, and what constitutes resolution of problems' (Taylor, 1991, 221) as keystone elements of the IUEs. These are summarised in Figure 1.1 opposite. The *sets of people* consists of groups that have some significant nominator, for instance an occupation that differentiates one group from another within the same category. This is an analytical differentiation, which targets the activities related to the nominator, and not all activities of the individual belonging to the category. It builds on 'assumptions, formally learned or not, made by a defined set of people concerning the nature of their work' (Taylor, 1991, 221). *Problems* are viewed broadly as questions, issues, tasks and sense making that the group finds important and typical as a basis for their activities at work. There are also ways of viewing or constructing problems in a certain manner that are shared among the particular group. *Settings* are seen as typical environments, consisting of both constraints and opportunities, with reference both to access to information and to domain of interest, which have over time developed into mundane processes of carrying out work. Finally, *resolutions* focus on anticipated responses to problems, that is, an understanding of what constitute relevant solutions to typical problems. All the constituents of IUEs that are related to each other through multilateral relationships; in formulating a problem, an anticipation of its resolution is already present as well as the affordances of the work setting, including views on which information is seen as valuable in any instance of work. Taylor (1991, 250) concludes that there is a need for 'rigorous flexibility' about the basic concepts within the field of workplace information, since concepts such as *information* can be viewed differently 'according to context and in the processes by which it

1. Sets of people	2. Problems
• The professions	• Not static
– Defined by formal standards	• Each IUE has discrete classes of problems
– Defined by problems and contexts	• Problem dimensions (examples)
• The entrepreneurs	– Well structured/ill structured
• Special interest groups	– Complex/simple
• Special socio-economic groups	– Assumptions agreed upon/not
• Demographic variables	agreed upon
– Age, sex, marital status, race	– Familiar/new patterns
– Socio-economic status	
– Education	
• Non-demographic variables	
– Media use	
– Social networks	
– Attitudes toward new technology,	
education, risk-taking, and innovation	
3. Settings	4. Resolution of problems
• Importance of organization style and	• Information uses
structure, if applicable	– Enlightenment
• Domain of interest	– Problem understanding
• Access to information	– Instrumental
• History and experience	– Factual
	– Conformational
	– Projective
	– Motivational
	– Personal or political
	• Information traits
	– Quantitative continuum
	– Data continuum
	– Temporal continuum
	– Solution continuum
	– Focus continuum
	– Specificity of use continuum
	– Aggregation continuum
	– Causal/diagnostic continuum

Figure 1.1 *Taylor's information use environments* (Taylor, 1991, 231–3)

becomes useful'. Furthermore, he opposes a rational view of decisions related to information use, 'as something formal, algorithmic, and thereby computable, excluding the importance of hunch and intuition based on experience and personal association' (Taylor, 1991, 250). There may be, however, different kinds of rationality actuated in decision making based on the distinctions of the IUEs.

This book

This chapter has focused on a number of aspects and prerequisites for modern workplaces, as well as a sample of frameworks that have been influential over the years and still today provide insights and guidance for research on workplace information. Outside the overview above, individual theoretical and empirical studies have contributed to a growing body of research; research into the work and workplaces of engineers and scientists has been accompanied by studies of many other knowledge workers and blue-collar workers, and research into information-related activities has now gone beyond searching for documentary sources (Case and Given, 2016). The review emphasises the importance of understanding what work is about in order to understand information acquisition and use as part of it. It also emphasises that there is no single framework or epistemological perspective that singlehandedly explains the entire phenomenon of workplace information, but rather that the different work situations are made of aggregations where information plays in from several perspectives. From the above classical frameworks on workplace information, a conceptual triplex of keystones emerges: *information* as (im)material entity, *individuals* as socially sited actors and *context* as a socio-historical basis for activity. Moreover, each keystone position possesses agency of its own, reducing the explanatory power of simple causal relationships, but not denying causal links *per se*. There is no united view upon how to define or weigh between the keystone conceptions; different definitions given, and emphasis placed on them, vary according to epistemological convictions and practical research interests.

This richness of views on workplace information leads to different understandings of information-related activities, such as information need, information management, information sources, information sharing, information production, information storing, information retrieval, information searching/seeking, information valuing and information use. Some of these concepts have been discussed since the beginning of workplace information studies, while others are new concepts coming from the latest trends and developments in workplace information environments. The richness of approaches and varying meanings for concepts can create deep understandings but also conceptual confusion. In this book, we try to provide some clarification, presenting discussions on important concepts within the area of workplace information, seeking to illuminate what is known, where diversity may exist and where fruitful research directions may lie.

Throughout the text we will illustrate the issues discussed through the use of personas, characters who represent working people within different work environments: Ann, a cardiologist working in a large urban hospital; Johan, a lawyer working in a law firm; Mary, a regional manager of a government agency; Bill, a coastal zone advisor; and Liila, a journalist working in a busy newspaper office.

All our five characters have intensive information needs and are part of complex and evolving information environments and their work displays rich information behaviours. Sometimes what they want from workplace information is the same, sometimes very different. As their story develops within the chapters we see how the many issues involved in workplace information affect individuals, their lives and their ability to perform their work.

The book continues with a chapter from Elaine Toms, entitled 'Information activities and tasks'. This chapter asks the big question 'what is work?', examining work as a concept from an information science perspective. The chapter presents a view of work as a series of activities that lead to a set of tasks and sub-tasks that are conducted to achieve an end-goal. This is unpicked through a discussion of three core elements of work: its information flows, processes and activities. The chapter finishes with thoughts on how 'work' might look in the years ahead.

The activities and tasks described by Elaine Toms take place within what she refers to as an 'ecosystem', a set of interacting people working within an environment created for the purpose of work. This important issue of the social, cultural and legislative environment in which we conduct work is taken up in a chapter co-authored by Gunilla Widén and Jela Steinerová on 'Information culture', looking at 'where work takes place' in the sense of the organizational context in which our work is performed. In this chapter they discuss how cultural factors affect the information behaviour of people in organizations, including the values, attitudes and practices of information. They discuss important concepts of information environment, information ecology and information climate, including common characteristics and differences among the concepts. They also discuss different levels and examples of information cultures, including connections with business success, information management, information practices and workplace information literacy.

As Gunilla Widén and Jela Steinerová observe in their chapter, 'Information culture is connected to information and knowledge management and gives a practical framework for developing management practices that support effective information use and knowledge creation.'

This concept of management – both in the sense of harnessing and making best use of our information and in the sense of human managers creating processes and structures within which we work – is one of the key concepts within workplace information research. Eric Thivant and Elena Macevičiūtė look at this large topic in their chapter entitled 'Information management', focusing on 'how do we manage our work information'. The chapter covers important concepts, including the personal information management of individual workers and the organizational approach to internal information resources as well as environmental scanning (i.e. the collection of information from the external environment). Importantly, the chapter clarifies the concept of information management and related concepts and presents core definitions and theories to explore the constituent parts of information management as an organizational activity.

Throughout Eric Thivant and Elena Macevičiūtė's chapter, and indeed throughout this whole book, we see reference to tools, objects, sources, people, etc. These are things to be managed, used, shared, organized, curated and learned about in order to 'do' work. The chapter by Katriina Byström and Nils Pharo looks at 'Information artefacts' or 'what information objects we use for work'. Artefacts are commonly defined as man-made objects for a purpose. In this case, the objects of interest are those that deal with information or knowledge, either by encompassing information or knowledge, providing access to information or knowledge, or facilitating production of information or knowledge. The chapter shows how information artefacts create complex phenomena that do not neatly organize themselves into straightforward categories or hierarchies. Understanding these artefacts from both a philosophical and practical perspective gives us a vocabulary to talk meaningfully about the information artefacts we use in our everyday work.

In their chapter, Katriina Byström and Nils Pharo state that 'Information artefacts…[are] chosen for use on the basis of personal preferences and expectations as well as socio-cultural practices', importantly noting that our choices of which information artefacts to use are not always simple and may be subject to personal biases as well as external expectations of how information is used. We can make choices about which information artefacts to use by the properties of the objects. Diane Pennington and Ian Ruthven focus on the concept of 'Information attributes' or 'how do we make decisions about information artefacts?' Information attributes are the properties of information and information objects that can be used to describe and differentiate information. Being able to differentiate information objects means we can select the most appropriate objects for our tasks and we can design information systems to organize and store information in useful ways. This chapter explains the background to information attributes and, with key examples, shows how information attributes can be used to design information systems and understand the decisions people make about information.

The final chapter takes one of the seminal models of workplace information, Taylor's IUEs, described above and mentioned within many chapters, and provides an expanded version of the model inspired by the contributions from this book. We also consider some of the cross-cutting themes from the book and point to future directions for workplace information as a research field.

This book originated through the work of the European Network for Workplace Information (ENWI). The network includes around 30 European members, including those who contributed to chapters in this book. All share an interest in high-quality research and practical development of information processes in workplaces within both the private and the public sector. We are grateful to the Swedish FORTE, Forskningsrådet för hälsa, arbetsliv och välfärd (Swedish Research Council for Health, Working Life and Welfare), whose support allowed the ENWI meetings to take place in 2012–16 (Project 2012–1481: European Network for Workplace Information (ENWI): Sustainable workplaces). We are also very much in the debt of the whole ENWI network for the stimulating discussions and fruitful sharing of ideas that led to this book.

Note

1 Parts of this section are discussed in more detail in Byström, K., Ruthven, I. and Heinström, J. (2017) Work and Information: which workplace models still work in modern digital workplaces?, *Information Research*, **22** (1), CoLIS paper 1651, http://InformationR.net/ir/22-1/colis/colis1651.html (archived by WebCite® at www.webcitation.org/6oJh1icrY).

References

Allen, D. K (2011) Information Behaviour and Decision Making in Time Constrained Practice: a dual-processing perspective, *Journal of the American Society for Information Science and Technology*, **62** (11), 2165–81.

Allen, T. J. (1969) Information Needs and Uses. In Cuadra, C. A. (ed.),
Annual Review of Information Science and Technology, 4, William Benton,
3–29.

Allen, T. J. and Cohen, S. I. (1969) Information Flow in Research and
Development Laboratories, *Administrative Science Quarterly*, 14 (1),
12–19.

Arshad, R. and Sparrow, P. (2010) Downsizing and Survivor Reactions in
Malaysia: modelling antecedents and outcomes of psychological contract
violation, *International Journal of Human Resource Management*, 21 (11),
1793–1815.

Barley, S. R., Meyerson, D. E. and Grodal, S. (2011) E-mail as a Source and
Symbol of Stress, *Organization Science*, 22 (4), 887–906.

Benselin, J. C. and Ragsdell, G. (2015) Information Overload: the differences
that age makes, *Journal of Librarianship and Information Science*, 48 (3),
284–97.

Boswell, W. R. and Olson-Buchanan, J. B. (2007) The Use of Communication
Technologies After Hours: the role of work attitudes and work–life conflict,
Journal of Management, 33 (4), 592–610.

Brennan, A. and Skarlicki, D. P. (2006) Personality and Perceived Justice as
Predictors of Survivors' Reactions Following Downsizing, *Journal of Applied
Social Psychology*, 34 (6), 1306–28.

Byström, K. (1996) The Use of External and Internal Information Sources in
Relation to Task Complexity in a Journalistic Setting. In Ingwersen, P. and
Pors, N. O. (eds), *Information Science: integration in perspective*,
Copenhagen, Royal School of Librarianship, 325–41.

Byström, K. (1999) Task Complexity, Information Types and Information
Sources: examination of relationships, *Acta Universitatis Tamperensis*, 688,
University of Tampere, Department of Information Studies, thesis for the
degree of Doctor of Social Sciences.

Byström, K. and Hansen, P. (2005) Conceptual Framework for Tasks in
Information Studies, *Journal of the American Society for Information
Science and Technology*, 56 (10), 1050–61.

Byström, K. and Järvelin, K. (1995) Task Complexity Affects Information
Seeking and Use, *Information Processing & Management*, 31 (2), 191–213.

Byström, K. and Lloyd, A. (2012) Practice Theory and Work Task
Performance: how are they related and how can they contribute to a study
of information practices, *Proceedings of the American Society for
Information Science and Technology*, 49 (1), 1–5.

Byström, K., Ruthven, I. and Heinström, J. (2017) Work and Information: which workplace models still work in modern digital workplaces?, *Information Research*, **22** (1), CoLIS paper 1651, http://InformationR.net/ir/22-1/colis/colis1651.html (archived by WebCite® at www.webcitation.org/6oJh1icrY).

Case, D. O. and Given, L. M. (2016) *Looking for Information: a survey of research on information seeking, needs and behaviour*, 4th edn, Elsevier/Academic Press.

Checkland, P. and Holwell, S. (1997) *Information, Systems and Information Systems: making sense of the field*, Wiley.

Choo, C. W. (2006) *The Knowing Organization: how organizations use information to construct meaning, create knowledge and make decisions*, Oxford University Press.

Daft, R. L. and Lengel, R. H. (1986) Organizational Information Requirements, Media Richness and Structural Design, *Management Science*, **32** (5), 554–71.

Deng, H., Karunasena, K. and Xu, W. (2018) Evaluating the Performance of E-government in Developing Countries: a public value perspective, *Internet Research*, **28** (1), 169–90.

De Solla Price, D. J. and Beaver, D. (1966) Collaboration in an Invisible College, *American Psychologist*, **21** (11), 1011–18.

Doss, D., Goza, R., Tesiero, R., Gokaraju, B. and McElreath, D. (2017) The Capability Maturity Model as an Industrial Process Improvement Model, *Manufacturing Science and Technology*, **4** (2), 17–24.

Dragano, N., Verde, P. E. and Siegrist, J. (2005), Organizational Downsizing and Workstress: testing synergistic health effects in employed men and women, *Journal of Epidemiology and Community Health*, **59**, 694–9.

Frey, C. B. and Osborne, M. A. (2013) The Future of Employment: how susceptible are jobs to computerisation?, *Technological Forecasting and Social Change*, 17 September, University of Oxford.

Fölster, S. and Hultman, L. (2014) *Vart Annat Jobb Automatiseras Inom 20 År*, – utamningar för Sverige. Stiftelsen för Strategisk Forskning.

Gerstberger, P. G. and Allen, T. J. (1968) Criteria Used by Research and Development Engineers in the Selection of an Information Source, *Journal of Applied Psychology*, **52** (4), 272.

Giddens, A. (1984) *The Constitution of Society: outline of the theory of structuration*, University of California Press.

Gorman, P. N. (1995) Information Needs of Physicians, *Journal of the*

American Society for Information Science and Technology, **46**, 729–36.

Hansen, P. and Widén, G. (2017) The Embeddedness of Collaborative Information Seeking in Information Culture, *Journal of Information Science*, **43** (4), 554–66.

Hayes, J. (2018) *The Theory and Practice of Change Management*, Palgrave.

Haynes, B. P. (2011) The Impact of Generational Differences on the Workplace, *Journal of Corporate Real Estate*, **13** (2), 98–108.

Hertel, G., Stone, D. L., Johnson, R. D. and Passmore, J. (eds) (2017) *The Wiley Blackwell Handbook of the Psychology of the Internet at Work*, John Wiley & Sons.

Huvila, I. (2011) Social Aspects of the Ecology of Information Work. In *Information Ecology and Libraries*: *proceedings of the international conference*, 10–12 October, Bratislava, 27–37.

Ingwersen, P. and Järvelin, K. (2005) *The Turn: integration of information seeking and retrieval in context*, The Information Retrieval Series, Springer-Verlag.

Jacobs, J. A. and Gerson, K. (2001) Overworked Individuals or Overworked Families? Explaining trends in work, leisure and family time, *Work and Occupations*, **28** (1), 40–63.

Jin, J. and Dabbish, L. A. (2009) Self-interruption on the Computer: a typology of discretionary task interleaving. In *Proceedings of the SIGCHI Conference on Human Factors in Computing Systems*, ACM, 1799–808.

Lave, J. and Wenger, E. (1991) *Situated Learning: legitimate peripheral participation*, Cambridge University Press.

Leckie, G. J., Pettigrew, K. E. and Sylvain, C. (1996) Modelling the Information Seeking of Professionals: a general model derived from research on engineers, health care professionals and lawyers, *Library Quarterly*, **66** (2),161–93.

Lloyd, A. (2009) Informing Practice: information experiences of ambulance officers in training and on road practice, *Journal of Documentation*, **65** (3), 396–419.

Lloyd, A. (2010) Framing Information Literacy as Information Practice: site ontology and practice theory, *Journal of Documentation*, **66** (2), 245–58.

McKenzie, P. J. (2004) Positioning Theory and the Negotiation of Information Needs in a Clinical Midwifery Setting, *Journal of the American Society for Information Science and Technology*, **55** (8), 685–94.

Mark, G., Gudith, D. and Klocke, U. (2008) The Cost of Interrupted Work: more speed and stress. In *Proceedings of the SIGCHI Conference on Human*

Factors in Computing Systems, ACM, 107–10.

Marks, M. A., Dechurch, L. A., Mathieu, J. E., Panzer, F. J. and Alonso, A. (2005) Teamwork in Multiteam Systems, *Journal of Applied Psychology*, **90** (5), 964–71.

Murray, W. C. and Rostis, A. (2007) Who's Running the Machine? A theoretical exploration of work, stress and burnout of technologically tethered workers, *Journal of Individual Employment Rights*, **12** (3), 249–63.

O'Leary, M. B., Mortensen, M. and Woolley, A. W. (2011) Multiple Team Membership: a theoretical model of its effects on productivity and learning for individuals and teams, *Academy of Management Review*, **36** (3), 461–78.

Ouye, J. A. (2011) Five Trends that are Dramatically Changing Work and the Workplace, *Knoll Workplace Research*, http://cbi-nc.com/2012/white-papers/FiveTrends_Workplace.pdf.

Paisley, W. J. (1968) Information Needs and Uses, *Annual Review of Information Science and Technology*, **3** (1), 1–30.

Paisley, W. (1980) Information and Work. In Dervin, B. and Voigt, M. (eds), *Progress in Communication Sciences*, vol. 2, Ablex, 113–65.

Parry, E. and Urwin, P. (2011) Generational Differences in Work Values: a review of theory and evidence, *International Journal of Management Review*, **13**, 79–96.

Rasmussen, J., Pejtersen, A. M. and Goodstein, L. P. (1994) *Cognitive Systems Engineering*, Wiley.

Salancik, G. R. and Pfeffer, J. (1978) A Social Information Processing Approach to Job Attitudes and Task Design, *Administrative Science Quarterly*, **23** (2), 224–53.

Savolainen, R. (2007) Information Behavior and Information Practice: reviewing the 'umbrella concepts' of information-seeking studies, *Library Quarterly*, **77** (2), 109–32.

Sloan, L. and Quan-Haase, A. (eds) (2017) *The SAGE Handbook of Social Media Research Methods*, Sage.

Stark, E., Thomas, L. and Poppler, P. (2000) Can Personality Matter More Than Justice? A study of downsizing and layoff survivors in the USA and implications for cross cultural study. In *Proceedings of 2000 International Conference of the Academy of Business and Administrative Sciences*, Prague.

Sundin, O. and Hedman, J. (2005) Professions and Occupational Identities. In Fisher, K. E., Erdelez S. and McKechnie, L. (eds), *Theories of Information Behavior*, Information Today, 293–7.

Taylor, R. S. (1991) Information Use Environments. In Dervin, B. (ed.), *Progress in Communication Sciences*, vol. 10, Ablex, 217–55.

Toffler A. (1980) *The Third Wave*, Bantam Books.

Veinot, T. C. (2007) The Eyes of the Power Company: workplace information practices of a vault inspector, *Library Quarterly*, **77** (2), 157–79.

Wajcman, J. and Rose, E. (2011) Constant Connectivity: rethinking interruptions at work, *Organization Studies*, **32** (7), 941–61.

Wersig, G. and Windel, G. (1985) Information Science Needs a Theory of 'Information Actions', *Social Science Information Studies*, **5** (1), 11–23.

Widén-Wulff, G. (2005) Business Information Culture: a qualitative study. In Macevičiūtė, E. and Wilson, T. D. (eds), *Introducing Information Management: an information research reader*, Facet Publishing, 31–42.

Widén, G., Steinerová, J. and Voisey, P. (2014) Conceptual Modelling of Workplace Information Practices: a literature review. In *Proceedings of ISIC, the Information Behaviour Conference, Leeds, 2–5 September 2014: Part 1*, (paper isic08), http://InformationR.net/ir/19-4/isic/isic08.html, archived by WebCite® at www.webcitation.org.

Wilson, P. (1983) *Second-hand Knowledge: an inquiry into cognitive authority*, Greenwood Press.

Wilson, T. D. and Walsh, C. *Information behaviour: an interdisciplinary perspective*, University of Sheffield Department of Information Studies, 1996.

Wilson, T. D. (2000) Human Information Behavior, *Informing Science*, **3** (2), 49–56.

2

Information activities and tasks

Elaine G. Toms

Introduction

In this chapter, we are concerned with 'work,' that is with 'activity involving mental or physical effort done in order to achieve a result' which is typically interpreted as the 'task or tasks to be undertaken' (Oxford English Dictionary, n.d.). In our information and knowledge intensive economy today, most jobs involve activities and tasks that create, manipulate, interpret and use information. In an analysis of job activities and tasks in the UK, Brinkley, Mardon and Theodoropoulou (2009) found that 60% of jobs required some to high knowledge content using primarily tacit knowledge, that is knowledge stored in the head (rather than codified knowledge). Nearly a decade later, we consider information activities and information tasks to be central to most of the undertakings within a workplace.

In this chapter, we deconstruct that work from an information-centric perspective. We start by examining work as a generic process involving a series of *activities* that drive *tasks*, sub-tasks and their associated human actions, interconnected in a hierarchical or network-like structure, that is the essence of what is done in the workplace. Next we consider three distinct but essential elements that affect how those activities and tasks are completed:

1 an *information flow* that emerges as streams of *data* and *information* from multiple units of the organization (both internally and externally), and upon which multiple actions may take place from the flow's origination to its destination

2 *information processes* that act on data and information while they are 'stationary', sometimes to create new information
3 *interactive activities* that involve people and objects (from informational to physical) working with information processes using that data and information.

Notably, all of these elements are deployed to service organizational goals and objectives.

One must not forget that work and its associated activities and tasks are not isolated and independent, but sit within an ecosystem – a social, cultural and legislative milieu (see for example, Suchman, 1987; Button and Sharrock, 2009) that is intersected by technologies and the work that needs to be done. That discussion is outside the scope of this chapter. In a holistic view of work within the workplace, we would need also to consider the organizational, functional and process workflow views as well as the information flow (Durugbo, Tiwari and Alcock, 2013) discussed here, and distinguish information processes from functional, behavioural and organizational processes (Curtis, Kellner and Over, 1992). But our focus is on the information work activities and tasks, and thus this chapter has isolated for further examination the threads that are the most tightly connected to that topic.

Data, information and knowledge – the fuel that drives information work

Intrinsic to work, and thus to each to these four perspectives, are data and/or information – the raw materials essential for work, and therefore the activities and tasks. Much has been written about the meaning of data, information and knowledge and, unfortunately, those words are often used interchangeably. For the purposes of this chapter, we have defined each of these concepts in a concrete way so that we can use the terms to explain the other concepts discussed in the chapter (see Marchionini (2010) for a good discussion of these terms). See Figure 2.1 opposite for an illustration of the relationship amongst the three, showing data as a set of numbers, characters and codes converted to information which is then integrated by workers with their existing knowledge to create new knowledge.

We consider *data* to be anything that can be expressed as a quantitative

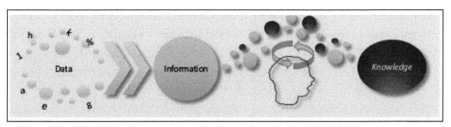

Figure 2.1 *The relationship between data, information and knowledge*
© E. Toms, 2018.

or qualitative value. Numbers, characters of text, audio signals and pixels, for example, are all data, merely signals that are looking for meaning. The digits '1 1 4 2 2 2 3 4 4 1' are simply a set of numbers, until identified as a phone number (in the UK), or a product code, or even a cryptic code used in a puzzle. Those digits (i.e. bytes) are raw or unprocessed data until we afford some sort of interpretation. With very few exceptions, most work involves using data that has already been prescribed a meaning using metadata. In the case of the example, the element, phone number or product code is the *metadata* used to describe the string of raw data. Most work will need the metadata (rather than the data itself) to make sense of the data.

Data becomes *information* when we interpret the signal, and ascribe to the set a humanly interpretable meaning (which is what metadata is). Those streams of signals or bytes may be used by multiple processes to create new information and reused in many different ways. For example, the data that represents an office address may be used by a delivery service to deliver an item, the fire service to assess its safety reach, the builder to reassess its building cladding, or a mapping service to map GPS co-ordinates to service locations in an app. This is the *information* that workers create, interpret and readily exchange. The boundary between data and information is very blurred and thus used interchangeably (especially in an era of 'big data'). In this chapter, data and information have been combined, with only the concept *information* used in referencing what is typically called data (i.e. anything in numbers or codes) and what is typically called information (i.e. anything in text, audio or video).

Knowledge, on the other hand, is the understanding that people have when they assimilate and absorb information and integrate and process it alongside existing information and knowledge stored in internal memory.

Knowledge 'empowers actors with the capacity for intellectual or physical activity' and enables them to think and interpret (Brinkley, Mardon and Theodoropoulou, 2009). Knowledge is the stuff encoded in the head, and may be either tacit or codified. Information, on the other hand, can be stored and readily communicated; its meaning is the interpretation or explanation that comes with it, or that an individual brings to it. Two people may not necessarily have precisely the same tacit knowledge about the same information event or object, although potentially they have or have access to the same codified knowledge – the recorded knowledge about that information event or object that is readily transferable (Choo, 2002).

While information is easy to communicate, knowledge, particularly tacit knowledge, may be difficult to pass on to others (and may leave a workplace with a worker's departure). For example, while the information may be readily available for using the new travel expenses reimbursement system, and an informative set of procedures may exist on how to use the system, one person (now on annual leave) may be the only one with the knowledge to deal with the idiosyncrasies of the system in concert with those workplace procedures. Thus, in this chapter we rarely refer to knowledge, as that will be the combination of information, skills and experiences that is intrinsic to the individual (and/or team). Instead we will primarily use information – codified knowledge – in discussing work.

In summary, in this chapter we think of data as simply streams of digits and codes, information as the meaningful data that can be recorded and meaningfully transferred from person to person and system to system, and knowledge as the unwritten and unspoken storehouse held by the worker.

About work and examples of work

Work has been conceptualised as 'a collection of tightly inter-linked human activities with explicitly or implicitly understood purposes, meaning, and values' (Huvila, 2008, 801). We often think of work as those undertakings that occur within the *workplace*, but any series of activities involving effort is work, regardless of whether that work is formally compensated or not. In this chapter, we focus only on work done in workplaces.

In the past century, work has evolved from a mechanistic approach (Taylor, 1911) to semi-automation (i.e. skilled), and now to augmentation (Davenport and Kirby, 2015). That early work involved managing primarily physical work that had been subdivided into discrete and highly structured, assembly-line style tasks. In the current information-dominated era, work is less physical, and more cognitively complex and intensive. It is supported by a range of technologies that vary from simple automation to perform basic tasks such as word look-up and calculations, to more sophisticated technologies that handle complex problems such as searching for fuzzy topics and running health economic models. The tasks left to people require more intellectual work, that is, require more conceptual knowledge and cognitive skills that aid human decision making (Vicente, 1999, 18).

In positioning the concept of work and its activities and tasks, it is important to think of it with respect to today's information worker, who arguably is anyone who creates and/or uses information to assist in making decisions and in problem solving. To explain the key concept, we relate it to two examples derived from an examination of environmental workers in government agencies. Each represents a composite of the role, i.e. a persona, so as to provide the richest examples to illustrate what we mean by information work. While their jobs are in environment management, the types of information tasks and activities that make up their work are not unlike those of many other office workers.

The first example represents a manager. Mary is a regional manager of a government agency that deals with environmental problems, and her core responsibilities concern operations at the natural ecosystem level. Thus, her activities include managing the staff who work with her on ecosystem issues; interacting with and supporting, technically, financially and scientifically, 16 community-based activist groups; setting priorities for ecosystem management, initiating action at the local level within her region, and formally responding to issues directed from the national level. Her activities range from developing policies and procedures to dealing with a wide portfolio of environmental issues, from aquaculture and offshore oil and gas to building dams, coastal erosion and pollution control. Given her role, she is often called on to provide 'briefing notes' – recommendations to the national level. All of her activities use data and information, and result in reports and presentations for local, national and international consumption. These activities generate a myriad of information processes that require digesting information provided by staff, which she has to integrate into a single report. Sometimes time is her enemy, as she has to deliver an evidence-based response to her superiors at the national level for political (and thus potentially public) use. These time constraints with partial evidence mean that she provides a 'best guess' based not just on the evidence but on her own knowledge developed from her years in the field.

The second example is a mid-level information worker. Bill is a coastal zone advisor who also manages a small staff, and is also required to work with multiple levels of government, and various sorts of local groups. Bill's activities are much more targeted and usually result from directives from his superiors. One of his most recent activities required that he assess the coastal setback problem in a local bay – that is, how far homes and infrastructures are located from the crumbling seashore and what the short-term and long-term consequences will be. He deconstructed this core activity into a number of tasks that included: finding the setback policies in other jurisdictions on the continent, using a number of data sources; identifying what scientifically is known about coastal erosion given the particular geophysical characteristics of the area, using scientific databases of research; finding the key geophysical parameters of the local area (e.g., bathymetry, and soil composition) using a number of databanks; and modelling various parameters such as wind and waves using modelling and data analysis applications. He needed to find all of this information before he could proceed. He evaluated his finds from authoritative sources, and quickly dismissed non-governmental reports that he thought might be biased. He did various types of data analysis, contacted reliable colleagues for expert opinion, and chased some probable and improbable leads. In the course of all these tasks, he made copious notes about these various information artefacts. To do this, he subdivided those four huge tasks into multiple sub-tasks (which he does almost in an auto-processing-like way). Using knowledge gained during his 11 years in the job, he integrated and interpreted the information from multiple sources to produce a set of recommendations for a possible course of action. Before he submitted his report, he contacted his trusted network for a second opinion.

Mary's and Bill's job roles define their core work activities, which are primarily, almost totally, information activities that use a lot of data, stored information and their own tacit knowledge. Their activities logically prescribe a range of tasks which in turn generate many different infor-mation processes that require interacting with many types of technologies, from searching in authoritative databases and serendipitous browsing and scanning, to note taking, data analysis and so on. All of these consume infor-mation, some of which is available directly using internal systems, and some they find externally to the organization. In addition, both communicate with other people, e.g. external and internal experts, and colleagues over the course of the work and also interact with a variety of types of technologies.

The workplace

We first start with the world in which work occurs, the workplace, which has been aptly characterised by Vicente (1999, 14–16) as having the following attributes.

1 It is composed of large, complex socio-technical systems (composed of people and objects).
2 Each system may contain many workers, requiring good communication channels and effective co-ordination of actions and interactions.
3 Each system tends to be heterogeneous in discipline, experience, background and culture, which thus impacts the common ground that workers need to share.
4 Each system maybe geographically distributed, separated by physical space and time zone.
5 Each system tends to be dynamic; some may require immediate response while others may have a lag time, so that a response for future action needs to be predicted.
6 Each system will have risks against which to mitigate; these may range from easy-to-recover-from, low-level risk actions and events, to those that may have devastating effects on public safety, the economy, the natural/physical environment, etc.
7 Each system uses some form of automation, because the system is so complex and the resource (e.g. data and information) needs so large that no single worker can directly interact with those resources and achieve the common goal; that automation will have built-in redundancies, imperfections and variability that must be monitored and controlled by workers.
8 Each system is unlikely to be highly structured, so that an element of flexibility is required to deal with unexpected events; each system cannot be characterised only by expected or frequently encountered events but needs to be flexible enough to deal with contingencies.

Each of these can readily be applied to the governmental agency for which Mary and Bill work.

This world is the one which shapes the work and its activities and tasks to achieve organizational goals. It is an 'information ecology' (Davenport and Prusak, 1997; Nardi and O'Day, 1999) interwoven with Taylor's 'information use environment' (IUE) (Taylor, 1986, 25–6; 1991, 218). Taylor characterised it as elements 'that (a) affect the flow and use of information messages into, within, and out of any definable entity; and (b) determine the criteria by which the value of the messages will be judged'. Vicente (1999) and Taylor (1991) concur on workers and the setting, and thus the context in which work is performed. But Taylor takes an information-centric approach in contrast to Vicente's ecologically driven perspective. However, it is generally agreed that the environment – the context or IUE – shapes and constrains how the work is performed and completed (see, for example, Stammers and Shepherd, 1995; Allen, 1996; Sonnenwald, 1999; Vicente, 1999).

What makes the workplace distinctly different from other types of IUEs is that the work system (and not the workers) determine the work goals (as argued by Diaper, 2004). The worker evaluates whether and when the task is complete, and decides on the best approach to achieve those goals. For example, if the work role requires a coastal zone advisor to recommend the best location for a power-generating wave turbine farm, it is the goal of the advisor's *work role* and not of the particular coastal zone advisor. Any other coastal zone advisor could have been assigned the same task. The same goal will be achieved, but the pathway for achieving it may differ, depending on each advisor's knowledge. In the case of our personas, each is assigned activities and tasks by their respective job roles or their line manager, but each will decide on how best to achieve the goals.

Deconstructing work

The next four sections will examine work, starting with the activities and tasks that make up work, and then examine the three interconnecting elements that are essential for those activities and tasks to be accomplished. In examining each, we need to note that each is ameliorated by the workplace context, the IUE, in which that work is performed.

Work as activity and task

As previously stated, all work is driven by organizational objectives and goals that are achieved through a series of *activities* — those that are defined within the scope of a worker's job description. When we typically think of work, it is this set of activities (such as Bill's requirement to identify and resolve coast zone issues, or Mary's setting priorities for ecosystem management) to which we refer. Activities are those elements at the highest level of task hierarchies (Norman, 2005) providing the goals for individual work roles, such as setting priorities for coastal management. Each activity necessitates one or more *tasks*, a concept that emerged from ergonomics and work analysis (see for example Taylor, 1911; Diaper, 1989; Vicente, 1999), and each task uses *information processes* (e.g. procedures for manipulating the information) and *actions* (i.e. low-level operations such as mouse clicks and keystrokes) (Norman, 2005). See Figure 2.2 for the relationships amongst these concepts.

Activities are always implicit in discussions of work, as they tend to emanate from the job description (although these are not considered in the Leckie, Pettigrew and Sylvain (1996) model of information use in the workplace). However, when we discuss work, we are more likely to concentrate on the task level — the operational level, which contains many

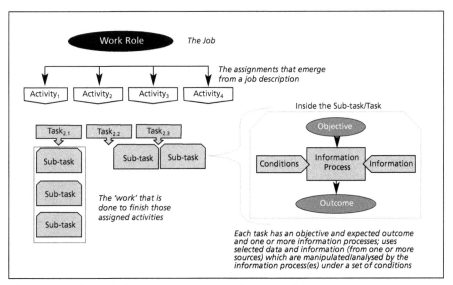

Figure 2.2 *The relationship between work role, activities, tasks and processes.*
© E. Toms, 2018.

instances of task, e.g. 'write a report on . . ., a letter to . . ., a proposal for
. . .'. A task may range from almost automatic processing requiring little
thought to very complex decision-making (Byström and Hansen, 2005).
We generally associate a task with its resolution and not with the actions
required to reach that resolution (Toms, 2011), unlike, for example,
mechanised work in which each action and operation is well documented.
In general, each task has a goal to be attained, and a set of instructions to
be followed (see for example, Hackman, 1969; Drury et al., 1987; Hackos
and Reddish, 1998; Byström and Järvelin, 1995; Freund, 2008). Each task
will use specific tools that drive specific processes, and use variable
information from particular sources/resources. Certain conditions and
restrictions may be placed on how the task is to be completed, or on what
an acceptable outcome is considered to be.

At its simplest, a task may contain a single action, which is mostly 'non-
decomposable primitives' (Sutcliffe, 1997, 39). Tasks such as 'What is the
meaning of the word *ecosystem?*' and 'Where is the location for Friday's
meeting?' are designed with a definitive path to a solution. Thus, at the
lowest level of a task hierarchy, each sub-task will be *structured*, e.g. enter
the keywords into a search box, press the submit button to perform a
statistical analysis. At its most complex, a task will need to be decomposed
into multiple sub-tasks that may be further decomposed into more sub-
tasks. At the very lowest level, the decomposition of a multi-part task into
these 'atomic units' will turn what appears to be an unstructured task into
a set of structured ones. Thus, in the most complex cases the solutions to
multiple sub-tasks may need to be integrated in order to finish the task.
Perhaps the best published example of a task decomposed into its
respective units is the analysis of the actions required in doing a functional
analysis of a gene (see Bartlett and Toms, 2005), which contains a set of
multiple sub-tasks, each requiring specific data, tools and processes.

In general, tasks may be considered structured or unstructured, and
instructional or constraints-based, as the examples in Figure 2.3 on the next
page illustrate. Structured tasks are primarily *instructional*, leaving little
discretion to the worker (Vicente, 1999) – for example, extract a citation
from the reference list at the end of the paper. Arguably, fact-finding and
word look-up are also tasks of this sort. But the tasks that use a *constraints-
based approach* (Vicente, 1999) are the ones that epitomise cognitive work,
and the ones that we most associate with an information work
environment. The 'answer' is not present in the head, and may not be

	Structured		Unstructured	
Instructional	Locate a map of the XYZ shoreline. Submit travel expense claim. Download and view the PDF version of the paper. What is the fish catch in the XYZ Bay?		Compare published policies on shoreline setback in clay-based cliff areas in any political jurisdiction. What is the best location for a wave turbine farm? What will be the long term effects of the oil spill in the XYZ Bay?	Constraints-based

Figure 2.3 *Structured and unstructured tasks.* © E. Toms, 2018.

readily available in any stored form; it may need to be created or calculated or interpreted from existing information in some fashion, as the examples in Figure 2.3 illustrate. Unlike those of an instructional type, the answer may not be definitive but approximated, and indeed may have multiple possible 'right' answers. In this case, usually only guidance on how to do the task can be provided, and a set of constraints or conditions focuses the task. These unstructured tasks require significant mental effort in combination with knowledge and skills.

When that very structured task is hierarchically decomposed into sub-tasks as illustrated in Figure 2.2, some of those sub-tasks may be unstructured requiring multiple interventions of human decision making. For example, one key sub-task in locating an ideal site for a fish farm is 'what are the characteristics of the bay?', which results in a further set of sub-tasks that identifies various parameters, from water circulation to habitat and recreational activities. All of these then need to be humanly explored, digested and interpreted, and merged before the composite task is complete.

From a worker's perspective, a task may be routine, repetitive and well known to the worker who follows a predefined set of rules – an internal procedure. Thus, regardless of whether it could be construed as instructional or constraints-based, it will appear to the worker as 'structured'. At the other extreme will be the non-routine task that is novel and perhaps performed only occasionally. On the surface it may appear to be structured, but to the worker, its complexity in combination with the worker's knowledge (or lack thereof) may render it difficult. Thus, a third element in considering task will be that level of complexity (Campbell, 1988; Wildemuth and Freund, 2009), which may be interpreted in two ways: physically (Gwisdka and Spence, 2006) and cognitively (Byström and Järvelin, 1995). Consider, for example, a task that may appear to be constraints based and unstructured, but is also routine to a worker. For our persona, Bill, this may be assessing a location for its potential for fish farming, a task that he has done many times for the environmental agency. This appears to be a physical and cognitively complex, constraints-based task. For him, this is a very routine, structured task, as it is something that he frequently is asked to do and now uses the tacit knowledge that he has acquired to develop a 'structured' approach for resolving it. Thus, we can classify tasks in a multitude of ways, but their accomplishment will depend to a large extent on the capabilities of the human worker.

While a structured and instructional task may have one or more specific operations before completion, unstructured tasks may have many possible pathways to task completion. The worker's knowledge and experience inform how the task is to be completed; and the worker ultimately decides that an 'answer' has been found. In the course of task completion, the worker may 'satisfice', when an optimal solution is not easy to establish (Simon, 1956). Constraints-based work allows for more variability in how the work is to be done and thus, more worker discretion in what makes for a good solution. As a result, different workers may not always use the same information or the same operations and processes for the same task and may achieve different but acceptable solutions. In a highly structured task such as 'submit travel expenses', or 'do a time-series analysis of wind and wave action', the procedure will be repetitious and invariant, and the solution always the same. In an unstructured task, the worker will use mental resources to engage in a range of human information processing, such as interpreting, calculating and comprehending. Such is the typical workplace problem solving when solutions are not obvious. For example, in the case of Bill, the coastal zone advisor, with the coastal erosion problem, the generic problem (i.e. coastal erosion) was well understood, but the most appropriate response with respect to the particular bay was not obvious, as each set of circumstances (e.g. clay versus rocky cliffs, weather patterns and wave action) varies from context to context.

Work tasks have been generically presented in a number of classifications to date:

- production tasks, discussion tasks and problem-solving tasks (Hackman, 1969)
- decision, judgement, problem and fuzzy (Campbell, 1988)
- administrative and communicative/facilitative tasks; information manipulative, analytic, strategic formulative/design; operative/generative tasks (Algon, 1999).

But, there is at present no standard, best practice in the classification of work tasks. In addition to the sets above, other task conceptualisations have been descriptive of the task, defining a characteristic of a task rather than classifying the task according to its intent. Consider Qiu's (1993) general and specific tasks; Kim's (2006) factual, interpretive and exploratory tasks; and Broeder's (2002) informational, transactional and navigational tasks, for example.

Overall, the tasks defined by work roles maybe primarily administrative, professional or managerial. Often some combination of the three may be found in the same work role. Administrative tasks tend to be structured, routine and repetitive, while professional tasks tend to be unstructured, requiring creativity, flexibility, problem solving, etc. Managers perform the greatest mix of tasks, contending also with the need for concurrent and interrelated tasks (Te'eni, Carey and Zhang, 2007). But the point they all share in common is the extensive use of information in order to achieve their goals. Within the workplace, these tasks may be conducted by the individual, or within work teams, or other work units, and thus the success of task completion may also be influenced by the human factor, e.g. extent of collaboration, type of leadership, organizational culture; the physical infrastructure, e.g. effectiveness of technologies implemented to assist the work, physical work environment; and the organizational structure, e.g. hierarchical, matrix (all of which is outside the scope of this chapter).

While the focus has been on information work tasks, the concept of an 'information task' has emerged also to reflect the number of variants on seeking, finding and using information. Today, it is difficult to find a task that could not be also characterised as an information task, which is rendering this concept somewhat redundant. The concept of search task is the best known of the so-called information tasks, characterised over the decades in a number of ways (see for example, Meadow, 1992; Marchionini, 1989; Choo, 2002; Ingwersen and Järvelin, 2005; Wildemuth and Freund, 2009). The distinction between an information-centric work task and an information task may be in the conceptual space in which the work is being done. Perhaps information tasks are generic processes that may be more associated with a tool, e.g. search engine, digital dictionary and reference recommender, rather than how those are deployed in particular workplace contexts.

Work as information processes

As noted in the previous section, tasks use one or more *information processes*. A process is defined as 'a set of partially ordered steps intended to reach a goal' (Feiler and Humphrey, 1993), such as doing a Google search, or analysing a set of data, or developing a reference list for a paper. Information processes, thus, are those actions and operations that modify and/or augment information so that the original unit of data or information changes in some fashion, or is used in conjunction with other units of data or information to create new information (Curtis, Kellner and Over, 1992). Information processing is generally associated with acquiring, recording, organizing, retrieving, sharing, displaying, disseminating and using information. The best known information process model is that of Choo (2002), who identified information processes at the organizational level.

Information processes delineate the procedural elements of a work task. The previous section discussed the concept of tasks in a generic fashion, although the implications were clear – it was all about the work, the substance of the organization's *raison d'être* – and we typically call those tasks 'work tasks' (Byström and Hansen, 2005; Ingwersen and Järvelin, 2005). All work tasks (at least in the context of this book) are also information-centric tasks that use information processes to meet the goal. An information process will use one or more tool(s) to execute that process. Finding the definition of a word, searching the web for information, analysing sets of data and monitoring the news on a topic are information processes that use as tools, respectively, an online dictionary, a search engine, statistical analysis application and news notification.

Characteristically, we associate an information process with traditional information searching or browsing. Information searching is usually interpreted as having three core sub-tasks: understand the problem; plan and execute; and evaluate and use (Marchionini, 1995), each of which may have additional sub-tasks. Browsing, on the other hand, is a non-goal-based, scanning process (Toms, 2000) in which people skim, select, examine and use or abandon (Bates, 2007). Both processes have defined procedures and sometimes the same tools, but they also differ on the presence or absence of a defined goal. Both are critical to completing information work tasks.

In addition to the searching and browsing, other information processes have been delineated, including:

- browse, chain, monitor, differentiate, extract, verify (Ellis, 1989)
- explain, stimulate, discriminate, orientate, etc. (Prefontaine, Bartlett and Toms, 2001)
- navigation, verification, comparisons, accretion, etc. (Marchionini, 2008)
- connection, suggestion, simplification, etc. (Gilbert, McCay-Peet and Toms, 2010)
- fact-find, how to, re-find, keep track, make sense, decision support, entertain (Toze, 2014)
- find facts, how to, make a decision, solve problem, learn (Freund, 2008)
- standalone informational, monitoring, sentiment/opinion finding, sense-making of conversations, people search, querying social network, refinding (Elsweiler and Harvey, 2014).

In general, information processes act on information to produce new information or identify information for use in another process. This is a classic but not exhaustive list of what we do to 'process' information in various work tasks:

(a) locate, collect, organize and store either temporarily or permanently for future use
(b) compare and/or link two or more documents or other information bearing objects
(c) synthesise units of data and information to understand something
(d) use in analyses, either or both of quantitative or qualitative, to summarise a large quantity of information so that it is humanly digestible
(e) create information from existing data, and/or modify, enrich and augment information to create new information

(f) monitor information about people, events and information objects, but not necessarily extract or filter the information

(g) integrate or combine in some way to deliver an 'answer', which may be a decision, a plan, etc.

(h) disseminate, including presenting, sharing, etc.

The two personas discussed earlier are actively engaged in these processes within their work roles. Searching for specific chunks of information, interlinking sets of citations and comparing the results presented in various documents are very typical of the processes they use to complete tasks.

Each process has a set of actions and operations. Arguably, search tactics (e.g. *find*, *reduce* and *block*) designed first by Bates (1979a, 1979b, 1987), and later modified by Smith (2012) specify what could also be interpreted as discrete but low-level processes that one would take in searching for information. Multiple actions such as mouse clicks and keystrokes are also used to activate the various processes.

The definitive set of information processes has yet to be conceived, but we can safely say that anything that manipulates data and/or information so that some sort of transformation takes place can be considered an information process. Here we think of task as having a specific goal, and these processes will be specifying the various procedures and actions that are required to complete the task and meet its goals.

Work as information flow

The concept of information flow is typically discussed in system-to-system or in person-to-person communication, but data and information can be considered independent of, and exist externally to, systems and people. Information flow is considered a significant part of all work flows (Al-Hakim, 2008). Think of the information flow from customer to waiter to the kitchen and back again in placing and filling a food order, which also includes the acquisition of the food elements and their processing. If we strip away the activities and tasks that make up work, we are left with information regarding that transaction as well as the meal production.

Within every organization is a stream of data and information intertwined across the organization that touches on every functional unit (e.g. human resources, finance, planning) within that organization (see for example, Nissen, 2002; Krovi, Chandra and Rajagopalan, 2003; Eppinger,

2001; Al-Hakim, 2008), and with constraints connects to external systems. Data and information both inside or outside the organization emerge from a source point or points and are transferred to one or more receivers. Both source and receiver may be a person or system, and the flow streams through an organization following formal channels, e.g. digital systems and their conditional structures, and informal channels, e.g. from person to person. Data and information may be created from within the organization, and merged with streams of data entering from outside the organization, such as specialised environmental data databases, technical reports, news feeds and social media. During and at the end of any activity the data and information may be stored internally, may be passed directly to clients and external organizations, or temporarily stored and/or archived in the 'cloud'.

Analogically, we can compare the information flow within an organization to a water flow or stream in the physical world. A stream meanders across the landscape until disturbed (or controlled) by stones and tree branches that divert the flow in different directions along distributaries. So too with respect to information flows within organizations. Stones and tree branches are now the people and systems that become gatekeepers (Allen, 1996), controlling for security, compliance and confidentiality (Blumenthal et al., 2006), and/or hoarders who block access knowingly and unknowingly (Lin and Huang, 2010). Maintaining reliability, credibility and integrity of the data and information stream thus becomes crucial to the subsequent effective use of that data and information by processes within tasks and activities. Mary, the regional manager, often had to contend with legislation that prevented the development of an optimal solution, and noted that colleagues in other branches of government would serve sometimes formally (with security status) as gatekeepers to information access, and sometimes informally, as hoarders to control the distribution of information that may give them personal power.

Along the flow, one or more transformations may take place when the data or information is plucked from the stream for use in different processes such as data analyses, data update/enrichment and data creation that are being performed to complete a task. Sometimes the same data is plucked from the flow to service different task goals, and sometimes that data is transformed and/or augmented before being replaced in the flow. For example, employee information retained by human resources moves along the flow for reuse by finance to reimburse worker travel expenses, and for use in annual performance reviews that re-enter the stream to update employee records. Thus, at many places along the stream, data and information may be filtered or extracted from the stream for integration or syntheses and used to complete tasks, from the preparation of contracts and cases by lawyers, to the analysis of time-series data and authoritative interpretations of research by environmental scientists. If the worker is restricted from accessing the data/information (e.g. lacks the necessary access privileges or security clearances), then some data/information will be 'lost' in the task completion. So when colleagues hoard the information, and systems put up artificial barriers to access, the flow of information internally is disrupted, and task completion can also be compromised. Consequently, how data and information flow within an organization can influence task completion, and thus is influential to how and whether an organization achieves its objectives.

Except for database construction, or data and information archiving, we rarely isolate data and information for this level of scrutiny. Data and information are mostly described as information resources or databases used by the organization, and simply taken for granted. But data and information have a life outside of those fixed units, and that life is dynamic, adapting to situations, and enhanced and augmented by work activities and tasks, sometimes automatically and sometimes with human intervention. Sometimes modifications to data and information may not be captured within the data flow, and may remain inaccessible in silo applications and technologies, or even inside a worker's head. Sometimes that data flow is subjected to reliability attacks that compromise the integrity of the data or information. When we isolate the data and information as a dynamic flow that interconnects all of the various functional units within an organization, we begin to see its full value as a critical and essential organizational resource – the fuel, that is fundamental to work, and thus also to activity and task, and not simply *just information*.

Work as interaction with objects

So far, we have viewed the workplace as a set of activities and tasks, as a suite of information processes and tasks; and as a stream of data and information used by those processes and tasks. Work activities trigger the need for a work task(s) to be done which in turn activates a set of processes which in turn activates a series of actions. However, all of these also involve a series of *interactions* between and among workers and objects (e.g. systems, tools, and content sources, cf. Chapter 5 on information artefacts). Without interaction, no processes or tasks would be completed and the data would remain in the stream. The process illustrated in Figure 2.2 could not be achieved.

Interaction is 'a special kind of action that involves two or more entities and a set of reciprocities that effect changes to each entity' (Marchionini, 2008, 170). This concerns the worker's engagement with the tool regardless of whether it is analogue, e.g. printed books and newspapers, or digital, e.g. desktops, databases and devices. The worker physically activates an element of the object, e.g. opens a book or selects a key on the keyboard, and responds accordingly to the object, as illustrated in Figure 2.4, human–computer interaction illustrating interacting with the device, as well as the content (information interaction) and showing the role of human information processing with that process. These sorts of transaction are repeated until the worker decides to stop. This process of interaction has been described as a 'Gulf of Execution', that is a two-part flow of information between worker and tool, in which the worker attempts to make sense of the interface to engage with the objects, and the 'Gulf of Evaluation' when the worker interprets the display and compares the response to the initial goal (Norman, 1986).

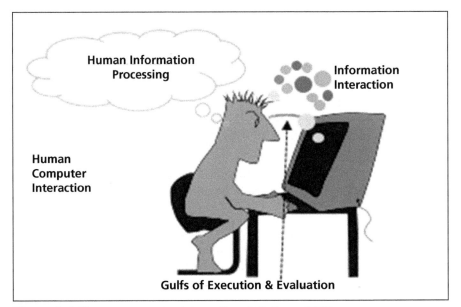

Figure 2.4 *Human–computer interaction.* © E. Toms, 2018.

In addition, this interaction involves and activates *human* information processing (as described in any typical cognitive psychology text) during which the human interacting with the object uses one or more senses, and interprets and stores the signals emanating from the object. This well documented human process is an internal system that controls attention, perception, memory, etc., so that the human's sensory system and its mental processes engage with the stored material, e.g. books, report, and eventually output a response of some sort. Today the human information processing system engages with a *computer* information processing system that takes digital data, and displays and/or transforms it into an output. Examples of these processes include information retrieval, data analysis and simple word processing. In an effective system, the computer information processes should simplify how much mental processing the human needs to do, and streamline the process. Accordingly, in the completion of any task, information processes activate a set of human and computer information processes, both of which work in concert to achieve the task goals.

Unlike the physical and sometimes mindless interaction with physical devices, information interaction is a more cognitively intensive type of interaction (Marchionini, 2008). In this case, the worker engages with the content of that object. It may be reading or scanning the print object. In the case of the digital object, the worker engages with the *content* rendered on the display, which may include reading and scanning as well as a number of computer input actions. In addition to reading and scanning, the interaction may include interpreting and using access tools, such as menus or search boxes, or examining semantic content, e.g. a contract, a database result display, a consultant's report. The success of that interaction depends on the affordances (Gibson, 1977) that the display (i.e. the interface) transmits, helping the user to interpret and navigate the various levels of the system. Likewise, the *textual affordances* present in the content provide a similar type of semantic cue that may act as a landmark within streams of content, directing the worker to view and interact with the content in a particular way (Toms, 2000).

This interactivity in which the worker engages with data and information within an information process is the essence of the work that information workers do. The processes are either formulated as a digital tool (e.g. search engine, web-based dictionary, e-mail, idea mapping), or packaged together in a suite of tools (e.g. data analysis software, office suite, project management, accounting). Thus the worker engages with the processes discussed earlier by interacting with a digital device. The distinction between the tool and what it does is now blurring with the emergence of suites of apps and likely this will continue as the device-function-information boundaries dissolve (Russell and Moskowitz, 2016).

This human–computer interactivity and the concept of information interaction (see for example, Marchionini, 2008; Fidel, 2012) have been well documented and researched. Workers bring to this interactivity their experience, skills and knowledge, which vary from worker to worker. However, they also bring some built-in human 'technology': mental models, cognitive and physical abilities, emotion, personality, etc., all of which also influence how the interactivity unfolds. In addition, attitude and 'digital dexterity' will also influence how effectively the interaction takes place.

How effectively that interaction occurs is not only up to the worker. Technologies that support and facilitate work are notorious for the variability in both their functionality and usability. While the system may be perfectly functional, it may be almost *unusable*, affecting worker performance and productivity in task completion. While an interface may appear excessively complex, it may be the only way to decompose a task into humanly digestible components. At the same time, software functionality and thus interaction are limited by human capability; human capability is about the same as it was a century or more ago, while technologies have reinvented themselves many times in the past couple of decades. An interface can only deliver what humans are capable of absorbing and understanding.

How does interaction fit with the previous three types of interpretations of work presented thus far? The worker interacts with an application that was designed to support the work task. The application extracts data and information from the data flow, and activates an information process. The worker interacts with the process (embedded as a computer function) to manipulate the data and information. Over the course of working through the task requirements, the worker engages with the content, recognising those textual affordances that direct attention. Depending on the complexity of the task, multiple applications (e.g. word processing, data analysis and project management) may be interacted with at the same time as the worker works through all of the processes required to complete each task/sub-task.

In addition to the interaction with devices, worker-to-worker interactions are conducted sometimes in person, and sometimes synchronously or asynchronously using a technology (such as telephone, messaging application or collaborative system) to facilitate and support the interaction. This interactivity is influenced by the work culture, social milieu and governance structure in which the workers are involved (cf. Chapter 3 on information culture).

Summary

The concepts that describe the undertakings around activities, tasks, processes, flows and interactions can best be illustrated by one of the personas. Bill, in his work role as the coastal zone advisor, has been charged with *activities* concerning the coastal zone, which include the impact of any man-made object or event on the coastal zone. This has led to his examination of the effects of introducing wave turbines in a local bay for power generation. He approaches this *task* by subdividing it into a number of sub-tasks, each of which uses a number of *information processes*, including extracting an earlier report that recommended this particular location as a wave power generation site; developing a simulation to ascertain future effects; comparing two simulation modelling techniques; extracting baseline data to feed the simulation model; using special monitoring equipment to monitor the fish movement in the proposed areas for use in his simulation; and so on. All of these processes extract *data* and *information* from existing databanks and databases, and all require *interaction* with a variety of tools and people, before the results from all tasks are integrated and interpreted, and a report is produced.

In information science, we have yet to articulate a clear framework for how all of these various concepts (e.g. activities, tasks, processes, actions, operations) fit together, especially at the operational level.

Conclusion

As pointed out in the introduction, we must not forget that this level of activity takes place within a large dynamic work ecosystem. How workers participate in activities and complete tasks varies with their experience and knowledge and their level of participation also changes with the intensity required to complete the work task. This may be exacerbated by the particular situation in which the worker is involved and the technologies that are provided to facilitate the work. Rather than the assembly line process we noted in the beginning, task completion in information work is fluid, with changing goals (see for example, Xie, 1997; Pharo, 2004; Hider, 2007) that affect how and when the particular task is finished.

The importance of data and information, and the source of that information, must not be underestimated. Without data or information, there would be no activities or tasks or information processes and no need for interactions, and thus no work. In addition, this entire operation is deployed strictly to accomplish workplace goals and objectives which are established, not by the worker, but by the organization.

This look inside what constitutes information work as product and production has illuminated the core elements contained in how we describe and research work. Task and activity are central to this analysis, but often information science, in particular, limits the study to information behaviour or information seeking and use. Yet work activities and tasks drive that need for information in the first place (Marchionini, 2008; Ingwersen and Järvelin, 2005). Except for searching and browsing, our previous research deals only in a limited fashion with information processes. We are more likely to think solely of information processing as a computer operation, or the substantive and well researched, cognitive perspective on human information processing. Yet those information processes are the critical procedures for manipulating and augmenting information, and form the foundation for emerging apps that focus on, in particular, unstructured tasks. We tend to think of data and information as omnipresent, but the way in which data and information have been used and abused by the tech industry (from Facebook and WhatsApp to Google and Amazon) has highlighted the life of data as a valuable essential resource and certainly has provided the evidence for data as flow and not as static resource. While human–computer interaction (HCI) and computer-supported co-operative work (CSCW) have provided the frameworks for how we think about interaction, their work has tended to focus on interacting with the technology. Yet we must not forget that information is an object with which we interact, and how we interact with information will be very different from how we interact with the tool that facilitates that interaction.

Future directions

Given the summary in the previous section, there is clearly scope for significant research in this particular area. But the research will need to be agile and nimble to keep up with the ever-changing technologies that stretch the research agenda and real-world implementations.

We are being challenged by seemingly annual technological developments, from cloud computing that is driving 'software as service' and work – anyplace, anytime – to the sensor-driven internet of things (IoT). Every action we take is being mined with deep data/text mining that has emerged to characterise even who we are as individuals.

At the same time, new developments in artificial intelligence (AI) and robotics promise to make work more efficient, effective, convenient and safe, and relieve the human of the drudgery of work – now a commonplace theme in the public press. The promise of these technologies is to extend a machine's role from that of a human apprentice to worker-machine collaboration – an equal partnership in the meeting of organizational goals and objectives. Forrester speculatively has proposed that we will advance to the integration of human brain with computers, or 'neural lace', a seamless blending of human capability with technology (Gualtieri, 2017) for a unified human–machine approach to task completion.

In future, these developments may be used to decide how work should (can) be allocated between human and robotic workers. In the not-too-distant future, robots will aid the human, and probably handle or partially handle much of this interaction. The current developments in personal digital assistants (such as Alexa, Siri and Google) for consumers foretell the likely developments that we can now expect to find in the workplace.

All of this begs the question about ethics and the value of being human within the workplace. We have yet to define where the human ends (or should end) and the machine starts in the production of work, or indeed who or which has or should have the overall responsibility. Will those digital assistants remain just assistants? This intersects with considerations for the workplace as an information ecology. What will be that social/professional interaction in a mixed human–robot world?

Technology is pushing the redesign of work. We are at a bit of a crossroads with respect to the pathway that we take, which will affect how humans work and indeed the involvement of humans in work. In an analysis of work in 46 countries McKinsey found that only 5% of jobs can be fully automated today, but that 60% of the jobs had 30% of tasks that were automatable based on current technological developments (Manyika, 2017). The 'sweet spot' will be in how information processes are automated and tools built to support and combine those features. Rather than waiting for the technological development, ideally we should be specifying the requirements for those information processes now, so that the technologies will fit and support human capabilities, and design the most effective ways of meeting organizational goals.

References

Algon, J. (1999) Classifications of Tasks, Steps, and Information-related Behaviors of Individuals on Project Terms. In *Proceedings of an International Conference on Information Seeking in Context*, August 1997, Tampere, Finland, 205–21.

Allen, B. (1996) *Information Tasks: toward a user-centered approach to information systems*, Academic Press.

Bartlett, J. C. and Toms, E. G. (2005) Developing a Protocol for Bioinformatics Analysis: an integrated information behaviour and task analysis approach, *JASIST*, **56** (5), 469–82.

Bates, M. J. (1979a) Information Search Tactics, *Journal of the American Society for Information Science*, **30** (4), 205–14.

Bates, M. J. (1979b) Idea Tactics, *Journal of the American Society for Information Science*, **30** (5), 280–9.

Bates, M. J. (1987) How to Use Information Search Tactics Online?, *Online* **11** (3), 47–54.

Bates, M. J. (2007) What is Browsing – Really? A model drawing from behavioural science research, *Information Research* **121** (4), www. informationr. net/ir/12-4/paper330. html.

Blumenthal, D., Campbell, E. G., Gokhale, M., Yucel, R., Clarridge, B., Hilgartner, S. and Holtzman, N. A. (2006) Data Withholding in Genetics and the Other Life Sciences: prevalences and predictors, *Academic Medicine*, **81**, 137–45.

Brinkley, I., Fauth, R., Mahdon, M. and Theodoropoulou, S. (2009) *Knowledge Workers and Knowledge Work*, A Knowledge Economy Programme Report, The Work Foundation.

Broeder, A. (2002) A Taxonomy of Web Search, *SIGIR Forum*, **36** (2), 3–10.

Button, G. and Sharrock, W. (2009) *Studies of Work and the Workplace in HCI: concepts and techniques*, Synthesis Lectures on Human-Centered Informatics, Morgan and Claypool Publishers.

Byström, K. and Hansen, P. (2005) Conceptual Framework for Tasks in Information Studies, *JASIST*, **56** (10), 1050–61.

Byström, K. and Järvelin, K. (1995) Task Complexity Affects Information Seeking and Use, *Information Processing and Management*, **31** (2), 191–213.

Campbell, D. J. (1988) Task Complexity: a review and analysis, *Academy of Management Review*, **13** (1), 40–52.

Choo, C. W. (2002) *Information Management for the Intelligent Organization: the art of scanning the environment*, 3rd edn, Information Today.

Curtis, B., Kellner, M. I. and Over, J. (1992) Process Modeling, *Communications of the ACM*, **35** (9), 75–90.

Davenport, T. H. and Prusak, L. (1997) *Information Ecology: mastering the information and knowledge environment*, Oxford University Press.

Davenport, T. H. and Kirby, J. (2015) Beyond Automation, *Harvard Business Review*, https://hbr.org/2015/06/beyond-automation.

Diaper, D. (1989) Task Analysis for Knowledge Descriptions (TAKD): the method and an example. In Diaper, D. (ed.), *Task Analysis for Human-Computer Interaction*, Ellis Horwood.

Diaper, D. (2004) Understanding Task Analysis for Human Computer Interaction. In *The Handbook of Task Analysis for Human-Computer Interaction*, Lawrence Erlbaum Associates, 5–48.

Drury, C. G., Paramore, B., van Cott, H. P., Grey, S. M. and Corlett, E. N. (1987) Task Analysis. In Salvendy, G. (ed.), *Handbook of Human Factors*, John Wiley & Sons, 370–401.

Durugbo, C., Tiwari, A. and Alcock, J. R. (2013) Modelling Information Flow for Organizations: a review of approaches and future challenges, *International Journal of Information Management*, **33**, 597–610.

Eisweiler, D. and Harvey, M. (2014) Engaging and Maintaining a Sense of Being Information: understanding the tasks motivating Twitter search, *JASIST*, **66** (2), 264–81.

Ellis, D. (1989) A Behavioural Model for Information Retrieval System Design, *Journal of Information Science*, **15** (4–5), 237–47.

Encyclopaedia Britannica (n.d.) Information Processing, www.britannica.com/topic/information-processing.

Eppinger, D. D. (2001) Innovation at the Speed of Information, *Harvard Business Review*, **79** (1), 149–58.

Feiler, P. H. and Humphrey, W. S. (1993) Software Process Development and Enactment: concepts and definitions. In *Proceedings of the Second International Conference on the Software Process – Continuous Software Process Improvement, Berlin, 1993*, 28–40.

Fidel, R. (2012) *Human Information Interaction: an ecological approach to information behaviour*, MIT Press.

Freund, L. (2008) Exploiting Task-document Relations in Support of Information Retrieval in the Workplace. PhD thesis, University of Toronto, https://tspace.library.utoronto.ca/handle/1807/16762.

Gibson, J. J. (1977). The Theory of Affordances. In Shaw, R. and Bransford, J. (eds), *Perceiving, Acting, and Knowing*, Lawrence Erlbaum Associates, 67–82.

Gilbert, S., McCay-Peet, L. and Toms, E. G. (2010) Supporting Task with Information Appliances: . In *HCIR'10, August 22nd, New Brunswick, NJ*.

Gualtieri, M. (2017) *The Forrester Wave™: cognitive search and knowledge discovery solution*, Q2 2017, https://techbeacon.com/sites/default/files/res136544_forrester_cognative_search.pdf.

Gwisdka, J. and Spence, I. (2006) What Can Searching Behaviour Tell Us About the Difficulty of Information Tasks? A study of web navigation. In *Proceedings of the Annual Meeting of ASIS&T*, **43**, 1–7.

Hackman, J. R. (1969) Toward Understanding the Role of Task in Behavioral Research, *Acta Psychologica*, **31**, 97–128, 162–87.

Hackos, J. and Reddish, J. (1998) *User and Task Analysis for Interface Design*, Wiley.

Hakim, L. (2008) Modelling Information Flow for Surgery Management Process, *International Journal of Information Quality*, **2** (1), 60–74.

Hider, P. M. (2007) Constructing an Index of Search Goal Redefinition Through Transaction Log Analysis, *Journal of Documentation*, **63** (2), 175–87.

Huvila, I. (2008) Work and Work Roles: a context of tasks, *Journal of Documentation*, **64** (6), 797–815.

Ingwersen, P. and Järvelin, K. (2005) *The Turn: integration of information seeking and retrieval in context*, Springer.

Kim, J. (2006) Task as a Context of Information Seeking: an investigation of daily life tasks on the web, *Libri*, **55**, 172–81.

Krovi, R., Chandra, A. and Rajagoplaan, B. (2003) Information Flow Parameters for Managing Organizational Processes, *Communications of the ACM*, **46** (2), 77–82.

Leckie, G. J., Pettigrew, K. E. and Sylvain, C. (1996) Modelling the information seeking of professionals: a general model derived from research on engineers, health care professionals and lawyers, *The Library Quarterly*, **66** (2), 161–93.

Lin, T., and Huang, C. (2010) Withholding Effort in Knowledge Contribution: the role of social exchange and social cognitive on project teams, *Information and Management*, **47**, 188–96.

Manyika, J. (2017) *Technology, Jobs and the Future of Work*, McKinsey & Company, www.mckinsey.com/featured-insights/employment-and-growth/technology-jobs-and-the-future-of-work.

Marchionini, G. (1995) *Information Seeking in Electronic Environments*, Cambridge University Press.

Marchionini, G. (2008) Human-information Interaction Research and Development, *Library and Information Science Research*, **30**, 165–74.

Marchionini, G. (2010) *Information Concepts: from books to cyberspace identities*, Synthesis Lectures on Information Concepts, Retrieval, and Services, Morgan Claypool.

Meadow, C. T. (1992) *Text Information Retrieval Systems*, Academic Press.

Nardi, B. and O'Day, V. (1999) *Information Ecologies: using technology with heart*, MIT Press.

Nissen, M. E. (2002) An Extended Model of Knowledge-Flow Dynamics, *Communications of the Association for Information Systems*, 8, 252–66.

Norman, D. A. (1986) Cognitive Engineering. In Norman, D. A. and Draper, S. W. (eds), *User Centered System Design: new perspectives on human–computer interaction*, L. Erlbaum Associates Inc., 31–61.

Norman, D. A. (2005) Human-centered Design Considered Harmful, *ACM Interactions*, July/August, 14–19.

Oxford English Dictionary (n.d.) Activity, https://en.oxforddictionaries.com/definition/activity.

Oxford English Dictionary (n.d.) Work, https://en.oxforddictionaries.com/definition/work.

Pharo, N. (2004) A New Model of Information Behaviour Based on the Search Situation Transition Schema, *Information Research: an international electronic journal*, **10** (1), http://files.eric.ed.gov/fulltext/EJ1082031.pdf.

Prefontaine, G., Bartlett, J. C. and Toms, E. G. (2001) A Taxonomy of Browsing Facilitators for Digital Libraries, paper presented at the CAIS/ACSI 2001, Québec, 27–29 May 2001.

Qiu, L. (1993) Analytical Searching vs. Browsing in Hypertext Information Retrieval Systems, *CJILS*, **18** (4), 1–13.

Russell, S. and Moskowitz, I. S. (2016) Human Information Interaction, Artificial Intelligence, and Errors, AAAI Spring Symposium Series, 21–23 March, Association for the Advancement of Artificial Intelligence.

Simon, H. A. (1956) Rational Choice and the Structure of the Environment, *Psychological Review*, **63** (2), 129–38.

Smith, A. G. (2012) Internet Search Tactics, *Online Information Review*, **36** (1), 7–20.

Sonnenwald, D. H. (1999) Evolving Perspectives of Human Information Behavior: contexts, situations, social networks and information horizons. In Wilson, T. D. and Allen, D. K. (eds), *Exploring the Contexts of Information Behavior: Proceedings of the Second International Conference in Information Needs, Seeking and Use in Different Contexts*, Taylor Graham, 176–90.

Stammers, R. B. and Shepherd, A. (1995) Task Analysis. In Wilson, J. and Corlett, N. (eds), *Evaluation of Human Work*, 2nd edn, Taylor & Francis, 144–68.

Suchman, L. (1987) *Plans and Situated Action: the problem of human–machine communication*, Cambridge University Press.

Sutcliffe, A. (1997) Task-related Information Analysis, *International Journal of Human Computer Studies*, **47** (2), 223–57.

Taylor, F. W. (1911) *Principles of Scientific Management*, reprinted 1967 as *Scientific Management*, Harper & Row.

Taylor, R. S. (1986) *Value-added Processes in Information Systems*, Ablex.

Taylor, R. S. (1991) Information Use Environments. In Dervin, B. and Voigt, M. J. (eds), *Progress in Communication Science*, Ablex, 217–25.

Te'eni, D., Carey, J. and Zhang, P. (2007) *Human Computer Interaction: developing effective organizational information systems*, Wiley.

Toms, E. G. (2000) Understanding and Facilitating the Browsing of Electronic Text, *International Journal of Human-Computer Studies*, **53** (3), 423–52.

Toms, E. G. (2011) Task-based Information Searching and Retrieval. In Ruthven, I. and Kelly, D. (eds), *Interactive Information Seeking, Behaviour and Retrieval*, Facet Publishing, 43–60.

Toze, S. (2014) Examining Group Process Through an Information Behaviour Lens: how student groups work with information to accomplish tasks, PhD Thesis, Dalhousie University.

Vicente, K. J. (1999) *Cognitive Work Analysis: toward safe, productive and healthy computer-based work*, Lawrence Erlbaum Associates.

Wildemuth, B. and Freund, L. (2009) Search Tasks and their Role in Studies of Search Behaviors. In *HCIR 2009, October 23, Washington, DC*, 17–20.

Xie, H. (1997) Planned and Situated Aspects in Interactive IR: patterns of user interactive intentions and information seeking strategies, *Proceedings of the ASIST Annual Meeting*, **34**, 101.

3

Information culture

Gunilla Widén and Jela Steinerová

Introduction

Information culture is a context-specific circumstance, affecting all information-related activities and practices in an organization. There are many tacit elements connected to information culture affecting workplace information practices. All our personas, Ann, Johan and Liila, have strong professional identities with very clear goals, work tasks and decision-making processes. They also have their individual preferences for e.g. information sources, and their information behaviour is affected by their demographic and socio-psychological factors. However, entering the workplace, there are organizational factors intervening with the individual ones. The workplace factors make a strong framework to which employees adapt, namely the information culture of the organization.

Ann, our cardiologist, is a social and outgoing person, and in her everyday life she interacts with other people as information and knowledge sources on equal footing. However, she works in a hospital where the hierarchies are very strong, where doctors are expected to make their decisions in consultation with seniors and peers, but not in discussion at length with the healthcare personnel, while social networks are mainly seen as time-consuming contexts. There she will adjust to the workplace traditions and use fewer social connections than she would in other situations.

Johan, our lawyer, is a person who likes to work individually and usually turns to a few reliable sources. He enters a new law firm where teamwork is a key value and the leadership style is to support interactive decision making. Johan will still prefer his individual working style, but will also with time adjust to the teamwork environment while everyone else is working in that way.

Liila, our journalist, is young and used to using social media for communicating with her friends and family. She also actively follows social media to keep up with newsfeeds on topics that are relevant for her work. At her workplace, however, the internal communication is done via e-mails and the weekly meetings are the cornerstone of sharing information with colleagues. Although Liila is used to instant information and knowledge sharing in her everyday life, she will learn to value the structured and in some ways slower pace of information sharing.

Having said that information culture is a strong framework to which employees adapt, the development of an information culture is a two-way interaction process. Individuals affect the culture and the culture affects individuals.

Defining information culture

Organizational culture

Organizational culture as a framework has long been an important field of organization study and there is substantial research on how the culture of an organization shapes the general behaviour of its participants. The interest in cultural aspects in organization theory was much highlighted in the 1980s (Schein, 1984) and since then has been a major approach in both organization theory and management practice, as it offers a framework for understanding organizational life at many levels and dimensions (Alvesson 2016). A much-used definition is the one presented by Schein:

> Organizational culture is the pattern of basic assumptions that a given group has invented, discovered, or developed in learning to cope with its problems of external adaptation and internal integration, and that have worked well enough to be considered valid, and, therefore, to be taught to new members as the correct way to perceive, think, and feel in relation to those problems.
>
> (Schein, 1984, 3)

However, there are many challenges when it comes to studying organizational culture, where not all artefacts and values are visible but rather invisible, unconscious and taken for granted without expression (Schein, 1984). This is still true today; it is difficult to define the borders of organization culture, its core and even its attributes. Still, it is a framework that helps us understand the deeper sense of an organization, the behaviour of its members and the practices that emerge over time, and has been used in numerous combinations, studying culture and performance, innovation, leadership and change, to mention a few (Alvesson, 2016).

Defining information culture

As a specific focus of organization culture, information culture is a concept mainly used in information science and information systems science to be able to focus the role of information in relation to different organizational activities and outcomes. Information culture focuses on organizational factors that affect the information behaviour of employees. The definitions are about what does the organizational context (culture) in which information is valued and which affects information behaviour and practices look like. In short, information culture is reflected in values, attitudes, norms and practices.

In the early information culture definitions, information was emphasised as an intellectual resource, equally important for business performance. For example, Ginman (1988) highlighted information culture as a culture in which the transformation of intellectual resources is maintained alongside the transformation of material resources. Later on, values, norms, attitudes and practices have been identified as important parts of an information culture, reflected in and influencing information seeking, evaluation, communication and use of information, as well as management practices (Choo, 2006; Travica, 2005; Widén-Wulff and Ginman, 2004; Wright, 2013). The information culture literature also acknowledges individuals' interactions with information within organizations (Wilson, 1997; Oliver, 2008) and focuses on the relationship between individuals and information in their work (Marchand, Kettinger and Rollins, 2001; Wright, 2013).

The role of information culture in decision making and its role for successful IT implementation has also been underlined. Curry and Moore (2003) emphasise the importance of an information culture in which the value and utility of information in achieving operational and strategic success is recognised, where information forms the basis of organizational decision making and information technology is readily exploited as an enabler for information systems.

Information culture is described as the contextual prerequisite for information management and information use. Information-handling skills and information use are shaped by how information is valued and how information processes are supported within the organization. How information is valued in workplaces can be based on relevance assessment, but information can also be seen as concrete assets in the organization. Values in information use in the workplace refer to autonomy, privacy, freedom of speech, copyright, universal access and accountability. Individual human values include privacy, trust, human dignity, well-being, intellectual property rights, access and moral responsibility. Interactions of values and infrastructures, and especially values built into technologies, lead to value-sensitive design (Friedman and Freier, 2005).

The definitions of information culture are summarised by Choo et al. (2008), who say that an information culture consists of the following components: communication flows, cross-organizational partnerships, internal environment (co-operativeness, openness, trust), information systems management, information management, processes and procedures. Studying these aspects and the outcomes of these processes gives a good framework for understanding the complex concept of information culture.

Related concepts

There are similar concepts of, and to some extent synonyms for, information culture, such as *information environment, information ecology* and *information climate*, also focusing on how environmental factors affect information handling in an organization.

Information environment

The term 'information environment' is close to the concept of information culture, connected to value judgements of information sources, information objects and people. The idea of information use environment was introduced by Taylor (1991) and refers to contexts of information use by different professionals (doctors or lawyers), depending on their problem resolutions, perceptions of information and decision making (Byström, Ruthven and Heinström, 2017). Information environment is explained as the entirety of information sources, consisting of information objects (databases, published documents), tools and services used for information retrieval, and management and analysis of information (Lauri, Heidmets and Virkus, 2016). Information environment in a wider sense can be determined as complex system of interactions of matter, energy and information in time in which the information process is manifested (Steinerová, 2018b). It is a part of the socio-technological environment, including the working environment and contexts of information use. The definitions and research on information environments focus more on the actual information landscape, the tools, objects and actors that are important within different kinds of information processes. They differ from information culture in the way that factors such as values, attitudes and traditions are not in the forefront.

Information ecology

'Information ecology' in organizations was determined by Davenport and Prusak (1997) as making information meaningful in information management. A number of authors have emphasised ecological perspectives as contexts of information interactions (Fidel, 2012; Huvila, 2008; Steinerová, 2010). Information ecology is a framework which aims at balance among actors, information and technologies in the information environment. There are several dimensions of information ecology: the horizontal dimensions, including information behaviour, information interactions, information management, information organization and use; and the vertical dimensions, based on different levels of individual, group, community, social and organizational levels and hierarchies of tasks. The ecological nature of information refers to such characteristics of information as reuse, different interactions (people, documents, information objects), diversity of information and actors, adaptations, products and services. Information ecologies are understood as dynamic places and spaces where people interact with information, information sources, systems and tools, e.g. hospitals or libraries (Nardi and O'Day, 1999). Connections between social and technological contexts represent information ecologies integrated into workplace information culture.

Information climate

'Information climate' is a related concept which describes information at work. It can be understood as a metaphor of natural climate, representing some stable traditions, norms and customs in information use in organizations. Information climate is created by a group of interacting individuals in a common frame of reference (Allen and Wilson, 2003). The core of information climate is represented by communication traditions, information practices and information use in organizations changing with the use of advanced technologies. The information climate concept is often connected to information overload as a challenge in business organizations (Edmunds and Morris, 2000) and the focus is on information infrastructures.

Information culture – factors and components

The common factors in defining information culture are represented by values, norms and attitudes, which in turn affect the information practices and communication flows in the organization (Figure 3.1). These factors are usually connected with information use embedded in work tasks, management, communication and collaboration. Differences in approaches stem from the emphasis on individuals (cognitive aspects), groups (collective aspects), communication (information sharing), and the information strategies of the organization. Information culture depends on further factors, namely whether the information is codified in documentation and guidelines, and how tacit information is transferred (e.g. training, mentoring, apprenticeship). Development of infrastructure can influence the information culture, such as the use of a corporate intranet. In other words, information culture is embodied in *information practices* in the organization, and can be managed through *information strategies* and *information policies* of the organization, where the components of an information culture should be focused.

For example, in the law firm, Johan, our lawyer, has advanced to senior manager and has acquired significant influence over how information is

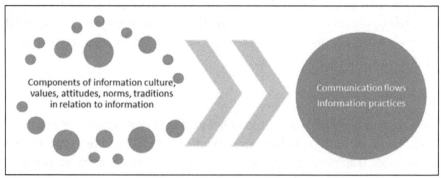

Figure 3.1 *Components of information culture affecting information practices*

valued and communicated. In the law firm information integrity is an important value. It means that there are some boundaries in information use which may not be crossed – especially misuse of trust or inappropriate use of information about the personal lives of clients. These rules can be informal or formal and it is clear that the wrong use of information will be punished. As a senior manager Johan has an important responsibility to communicate the importance of these rules, himself working in line with the rules, showing examples of respecting the information strategy, policy and values of the firm. In that way the information culture is visibly communicated in the firm, although many tacit elements are involved.

There are different kinds of information cultures. In order to be able to manage the information culture it is important to be aware of the values, attitudes and norms that shape the culture in the particular organization. The hierarchical model is based on a hierarchy of information flows. Sometimes it is called the command-and-control type of organizational culture. Other types of organizations emphasise and value information in all their communicative and business processes. Managers promote the flow of information across all the divisions horizontally, across boundaries of departments, with bottom-up production of ideas and innovations. Types of information cultures can also be divided into open and closed, internally or externally focused, controlling and empowering (Davenport and Prusak, 1997). Different types of information cultures also have effects on the performance of the organization's activities (Widén-Wulff, 2005). Our journalist Liila works in a media house with a so-called open information culture. The employees are well informed about the activities in different departments, they are happy to share information and tips with each other and they see shared information as a strength rather than keeping information and knowledge to themselves. This minimises the time spent in seeking external information and there is less information seeking happening in parallel. Ann, our cardiologist, works in a hierarchical and closed information culture. Information for treating patients is shared according to formal protocols and works well, but a lot of time is consumed in seeking externally located information about more general issues when information is not shared between units in the hospital.

Information culture is difficult to change while embedded in values, attitudes and traditions. One way of managing the information culture is to develop and adapt strategies and policies that focus on information processes and information work. In these strategies it is important to focus on the cultural elements, namely values. Leading values is probably the most efficient way to get closer to changing an existing information culture. A further step in managing information and information culture is the way managers communicate with other employees: whether they report on mistakes and failures and build trust and whether they are willing to provide others with information in collaborative ways. As a senior manager, Johan now has an opportunity to affect the information culture of the firm. He personally prefers to work individually and will probably, within the framework of teamwork, which is a key value of the firm, bring in some of his preferences and support an individual working style as a complement to interactive decision making. As a senior manager he is a role model for other employees: he has to promote appropriate information use to other people. In this sense he uses information for self-efficacy (personal involvement and organization). Although Johan has slightly different priorities in a collaborative working style, he would not have been selected as a senior manager if the top management did not believe that he still respects the key values of the firm, emphasising teamwork and information transparency.

Information culture can be used to manage information processes, but it can also be used as a framework to understand information use and information practices in an organization. In a study by Nordsteien and Byström (2018) it is shown that when new healthcare professionals interact with the information practices and information culture of the organization, contradictions between formal and informal practices are brought to the fore. Individual and organizational information practices must be renegotiated, leading to a dynamic development of these practices. Information practices are manifested in a broad range of social and technological activities. The challenge is the use of information and communication technologies and readjustment of digital skills, information skills and communication and collaboration processes (Lloyd, 2017). The cultural dimension explains how information is valued and what kinds of attitudes and norms exist in connection to information sharing and seeking. This can help to understand which information sources are prioritised, or other patterns of information behaviour in an organization (Bergeron et al., 2007; Choo et al., 2008, Vick, Nagano and Popadiuk, 2015).

Information use means applying information to work tasks in order to solve problems and take decisions. Information use is based on traditions of handling information in organizations and can lead to creation of information products or services. Information uses again have impact on information culture in building best practices, communities of practice, use of information resources and strategies of information seeking. For example, it is necessary that the use of information should add value to the work and outcomes of employees. Business managers in private companies need the right information to achieve business outcomes (financial, legal procedures), but also to adopt new practices and innovations (data about clients, competitors, transfer of new practices, case studies). External information is needed for introducing new products and services, experimenting with innovations, evaluation of good practices or creating new knowledge. Awareness of information resources and control and monitoring of the information environment are typical information practices of managers (Cheuk, 2017). These practices are important in forming the information culture of the company. How information is valued in the processes is crucial for how effectively information flows in the company.

We can conclude that information culture depends on the type of organization, types of workers and types of their roles and tasks. In different information cultures values are embedded in best practices, experience and communities of practice.

Information culture research

There are a few studies looking at information culture at the level of society (e.g. Menou, 2002; Tredinnick, 2008), discussing policies and strategies in the digital age. The main focus, however, has been at the organizational level and information culture has been used as a framework in studying both private and public organizations. A variety of organizations have been studied from an information culture point of view, e.g. insurance companies, municipalities, law firms and archives. In organization theory Schein (1984) emphasises that to study an organization's culture a complex study design is needed, including interviews, observations and joint-inquiry approaches. It is also important to study a large number of organizations. This is also put forward in Hansen and Widén (2017), where two frameworks of workplace information research are discussed: information culture and collaborative information seeking. Bringing these two frameworks closer together brings a more holistic approach to complex information processes. How well collaborative information-seeking processes in a workplace function depends a lot on what kind of information culture exists in that workplace or within a team. Combining frameworks bring new dimensions, and research into information culture benefits especially from focusing on different perspectives. There is a so-called chicken-and-egg situation: cultural elements affect information practices and information practices affect the culture.

In the following sections we will highlight information culture research and categorise it according to the main perspectives used in this area of research.

Information culture and business success

A traditional approach in information culture research has been to study the connection between information culture and business performance. Different types of information cultures have been identified and the impact on work processes is clear. For example, an information culture that is in line with the organization's overall strategy and beliefs is expected to be more efficient and supports business success. An open information culture reflects a more communicative attitude in the organization and fits better when the organization is in a developing phase (Widén-Wulff, 2005; Choo, 2013). Organizations need to be aware of their information culture profiles to manage information work efficiently.

Information culture and information management

As stated above, it is important to understand the organization's information culture from a management point of view; this has also been a study approach within information culture research (Choo, 2013; Svärd, 2013; Travica, 2008). Information culture is connected to information and knowledge management and gives a practical framework for developing management practices that support effective information use and knowledge creation. Research has focused on the importance of including all layers of relationships (Figure 3.2 opposite) between information culture and information management to make the most of information and knowledge as a resource.

A mature and enabling information culture better supports the adoption of e.g. new information systems and technologies. The key issue is not the technology in itself but the social factors affecting individual information capabilities (Orlikowski, 2010). Information culture in organizations can

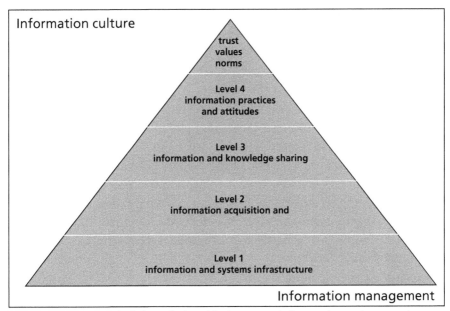

Figure 3.2 *Pyramid of the relationship between information culture and information management.* Modified from Hawamdeh (2005).

determine whether the same information system or web service is adopted successfully or not (Davenport and Prusak, 1997). The decisive factors are traditions, information behaviour patterns, communication patterns, intergenerational relationships, norms and values assigned to information sharing and information use. Depending on adoption of technologies we can discern early adopters and late adopters (Borgman, 2007), and balanced and imbalanced information ecologies (based on the degree of attention paid to single components, such as ICT).

Future directions of information culture research

Information at work is changing constantly and fairly rapidly. For example, today's workplace is increasingly digital and fragmented and people work in organizations where they are not physically located in the same facilities. These circumstances are challenging for developing a common information culture framework, shared values and common information practices. It would be important to address these kinds of new working environments also with an information culture perspective to see whether the development of an information culture is different in online work settings and how information culture could support efficient information sharing in such environments. Another important perspective in this context is how professional information literacy is developed in digital (web) environments (Abdi and Bruce, 2015). In academic workplaces the study of information practices of researchers in workplace information ecologies has recently been introduced (Steinerová, 2018a).

An ongoing concern in relation to information at work is information overload. Research in the late 1990s had already highlighted that good management strategies, communication, trust and information sharing can help ease the information overload of workers (Davenport and Prusak, 1997). Although this has long been a concern and a research topic, it still needs to be emphasised while information constantly changes forms and formats. It is important to foster an information culture that supports ongoing development in making information meaningful by providing context, information pruning, enhancing the style of information and choosing the right medium.

Information culture is much studied in connection with management, but less in relation to leadership. Leadership aspects and how they affect information handling would be important to study, to reach a more holistic understanding and help us design more concrete implementation and assessment frameworks in relation to information-handling skills in the workplace. Quantitative studies measuring the relationship between leadership and information-handling skills would also be welcome; most information culture studies so far have used a qualitative approach (Widén and Karim, 2017).

The changing information environment puts special emphasis on employees' skills in managing their own information processes. During the last few years there has been a growing interest in understanding individuals' information literacy in a workplace context. Information culture constitutes the background for the use of workplace information resources, for information practices and learning. Advances in workplace information literacy are based on social networks, collaboration, management of communications and transfer of skills (Abram, 2013). How workers use and experience information are dependent on or shaped by the context, such as work tasks, on-the-job experiences and social aspects. This means that the role of an organization's information culture would be expected to influence the development of workplace information literacy. This connection has not, however, been explored previously (Widén and Karim, 2017), although new concepts and new perspectives are emerging in the relations between workplace and information literacy (Forster, 2017; Lloyd, 2010). The information culture perspective could add multiple social and cultural factors to the discussion of workplace information literacy, which is not an individual attribute or set of activities, but rather a collective attempt in performing tasks at workplaces. Individual information-handling skills should be supported in interaction with the workplace information culture.

The conceptual analysis of workplace information, presented in the framework of the ENWI project (Widén, Steinerová and Voisey, 2014), underlined the complexity in studying information and the importance of focusing contextual factors such as information culture. Both individual and collective factors of experience in communities and disciplines are taken into account, especially social practices of collaboration and information sharing. An information culture approach would be beneficial in connection to workplace learning, focusing on values and attitudes, but has not been studied so far to any large extent.

Conclusions

Information culture is about values and attitudes to information, it is about norms and traditions, shaping the information practices of an organization. Ann, Johan and Liila are all affected by the information culture of their workplaces, but are also contributing to the development of their particular information cultures through their individual actions and priorities. Research and practice, however, show that the cultural factors of an organization are usually stronger than the individual information behaviour of the employees, meaning that managing information practices should be done through communicating values, norms and traditions. Information culture is a decisive factor in efficient information use and adoption of information technologies in organizations. Information culture can be both a prerequisite as well as a barrier to efficient information and knowledge management.

Information culture provides a broad view of several contexts of information use environments, focused on human information processing. It connects technologies, people and information environments in a framework of values, attitudes and traditions. Apart from information culture, there are several related concepts, such as information environment, information climate and information ecology. The changing nature of work will lead to distributed networking of work, new technologies and social software, demand for new work and information skills, and demand for more sustainable organizations. New information practices as well as new professions of digital librarians, data curators and information architects will emerge. Shaping information cultures that support new and hybrid workplaces with flexible work styles will be crucial, yet challenging while an information culture is difficult to change. Studying information culture is therefore important, so as to be aware of factors shaping and affecting it, enabling it to be as adaptive as possible.

References

Abdi, E. S. and Bruce, C. (2015) From Workplace to Professions: new focus for the information literacy discourse. In: *Information Literacy: moving toward sustainability*, ECIL 2015, CCIS 552, Springer, 59–69.

Abram, S. (2013) Workplace Information Literacy: it's different. In Hepworth, M. and Walton, G. (eds), *Developing People's Information Capabilities: fostering information literacy in educational workplace and community contexts*, Emerald, 205–22.

Allen, D. K. and Wilson, T. D. (2003) Information Overload: context and causes, *New Review of Information Behaviour Research*, 4, 31–44.

Alvesson, M. (2016) Organization Culture and Work. In Edgell, S., Gottfried, H. and Granter, E. (eds), *The Sage Handbook of Sociology of Work and Employment*, Sage, 262–82.

Bergeron, P., Heaton, L., Choo, C. W., Detlor, B., Bouchard, D. and Paquette, S. (2007) Knowledge and Information Management Practices in Knowledge-intensive Organizations: a case study of a Quebec public health management organization. In Arsenault, C. and Dalkir, K. (eds), *Information Sharing in a Fragmented World: crossing boundaries*, McGill University, Canadian Association for Information Science (CAIS/ACSI) 35th Annual Conference, https://journals.library.ualberta.ca/ojs.cais-acsi.ca/index.php/cais-asci/article/view/200/162.

Borgman, C. (2007) *Scholarship in the Digital Age: information, infrastructure and the internet*, MIT Press, 336.

Byström, K., Ruthven, I. and Heinström, J. (2017) Work and Information: which workplace models still work in modern digital workplaces? *Information Research*, 22 (1), CoLIS paper 1651, http://InformationR.net/ir/22-1/colis/colis1651.html.

Cheuk, B. (2017) The 'Hidden' Value of Information Literacy in the
Workplace Context: how to unlock and create value. In: Forster, M. (ed.),
Information Literacy in the Workplace, Facet Publishing, 131–47.

Choo, C. W. (2006) *The Knowing Organization: how organizations use
information to construct meaning, create knowledge, and make decisions*,
2nd edn, Oxford University Press.

Choo, C. W. (2013) Information Culture and Organizational Effectiveness,
International Journal of Information Management, **33** (5), 775.

Choo, C. W., Bergeron, P., Detlor, B., and Heaton, L. (2008) Information
Culture and Information Use: an exploratory study of three organizations,
Journal of the American Society for Information Science and Technology, **59**
(5), 792–804.

Curry, A. and Moore, C. (2003) Assessing Information Culture: an exploratory
model, *International Journal of Information Management*, **23** (2), 91–110.

Davenport, T. H. and Prusak, L. (1997) *Information Ecology: mastering the
information and knowledge environment*, Oxford University Press.

Edmunds, A. and Morris, A. (2000) The Problem of Information Overload in
Business Organizations: a review of the literature, *International Journal of
Information Management*, **20**, 17–28.

Fidel, R. (2012) *Human Information Interaction: an ecological approach to
information behavior*, MIT Press.

Forster, M. (2017) *Information Literacy in the Workplace*, Facet Publishing.

Friedman, B. and Freier, N. G. (2005) Value Sensitive Design. In *Theories of
Information Behavior*, Information Today, 368–72.

Ginman, M. (1988) Information Culture and Business Performance, *IATUL
Quarterly*, **2** (2), 93–106.

Hansen, P. and Widén, G. (2017) The Embeddedness of Collaborative
Information Seeking in Information Culture, *Journal of Information Science*,
43 (4), 554–66.

Hawamdeh, S. (ed.) (2005) *Knowledge Management: nurturing culture,
innovation and technology*, World Scientific, vi.

Huvila, I. (2008) Information Work Analysis: an approach to research on
information interactions and information behaviour in context, *Information
Research*, **13** (3), paper 349, http://InformationR.net/ir/13–
3/paper349.html.

Lauri, L., Heidmets, M. and Virkus, S. (2016) The Information Culture of
Higher Education Institutions: the Estonian case, *Information Research*, **21**
(3), paper 722, http://InformationR.net/ir/21-3/paper722.html, archived

by WebCite® at www.webcitation.org/6kRgK9BTZ.

Lloyd, A. (2010) *Information Literacy Landscapes: information literacy in education, workplace and everyday contexts*, Elsevier.

Lloyd, A. (2017) Learning Within for Beyond: exploring a workplace information literacy design. In Forster, M. (ed.), *Information Literacy in the Workplace*, Facet Publishing, 97–112.

Marchand, D., Kettinger, W. and Rollins, J. (2001) *Information Orientation: the link to business performance*, Oxford University Press.

Menou, M. (2002) *Information Literacy in National Information and Communications Technology (ICT) Policies: the missed dimension, information culture*, www.ictliteracy.info/rf.pdf/The%20Missed%20Dimension.pdf.

Nardi, B. A. and O'Day, V. L. (1999) *Information Ecologies: using technology with heart*, MIT Press.

Nordsteien, A. and Byström, K. (2018) Transitions in Workplace Information Practices and Culture: the influence of newcomers on information use in healthcare, *Journal of Documentation*, **74** (4), 827–43.

Oliver, G. (2008) Information Culture: exploration of differing values and attitudes to information in organizations, *Journal of Documentation*, **64** (3), 363–85.

Orlikowski, W. J. (2010) The Sociomateriality of Organizational Life: considering technology in management research, *Cambridge Journal of Economics*, **34** (1), 125–41.

Schein, E. H. (1984) Coming to a New Awareness of Organizational Culture, *Sloan Management Review*, **25** (2), 3–16.

Steinerová, J. (2010) Ecological Dimensions of Information Literacy, *Information Research*, **15** (4) paper colis719, http://InformationR.net/ir/15-4/colis719.html.

Steinerová, J. (2018a) Information Literacy Practices of Researchers in Workplace Information Ecologies. In: S. Kurbanoglu et al. (eds), *Information Literacy in the Workplace*, Springer, 30–40, https://doi.org/10.1007/978-3-319-74334-9.

Steinerová, J. (2018b) *Informa né Prostredie a Vedecká Komunikácia: informa né ekológie (Information Environment and Scholarly Communication: information ecologies)*, Univerzita Komenského.

Svärd, P. (2013) Enterprise Content Management and the Records Continuum Model as Strategies for Long-term Preservation of Digital Information, *Records Management Journal*, **23** (3), 159–76.

Taylor, R. S. (1991) Information Use Environments. In Dervin, B. (ed.), *Progress in Communication Sciences*, Vol. 10, Ablex, 217–55.

Travica, B. (2005) Information Politics and Information Culture: a case study, *Informing Science: the international journal of an emerging transdiscipline*, **8**, 211–44.

Travica, B. (2008) Influence of Information Culture on Adoption of a Self-service System, *Journal of Information, Information Technology, and Organizations*, **3** (1), 1–15.

Tredinnick, L. (2008) *Digital Information Culture*, Chandos.

Vick, T. E., Nagano, M. S. and Popadiuk, S. (2015) Information Culture and its Influences in knowledge Creation: evidence from university teams engaged in collaborative innovation projects, *International Journal of Information Management*, **35** (3), 292–8.

Widén, G., Steinerová, J. and Voisey, P. (2014) Conceptual Modelling of Workplace Information Practices: a literature review, *Information Research, Proc. of ISIC, Leeds, 2–5 September 2014: Part 1*, paper isic08, http://InformationR.net/ir/19-4/isic/isic08.html.

Widén, G. and Karim, M. (2017) Role of Information Culture in Workplace Information Literacy: a literature review. In *Proceedings of the ECIL2017 conference, Saint-Malo, France, 18–21 September 2017*.

Widén-Wulff, G. (2005) Business Information Culture: a qualitative study. In: Macevičiūtė, E. and Wilson, T. D. (eds), *Introducing Information Management: an information research reader*, Facet Publishing, 31–42.

Widén-Wulff, G. and Ginman, M. (2004) Explaining Knowledge Sharing in Organizations Through the Dimensions of Social Capital, *Journal of Information Science*, **30** (5), 448–58, doi: 10.1177/0165551504046997.

Wilson, T. (1997) Information Behavior: an interdisciplinary perspective, *Information Processing and Management*, **33** (4), 551–72.

Wright, T. (2013) Information Culture in a Government Organization, *Records Management Journal*, **23** (1), 14–36.

4

Information management

Elena Macevičiūtė and Eric Thivant

Introduction

This chapter discusses information management at the workplace It includes the *personal information management* of individual workers and the organizational approach to internal information resources, as well as environmental scanning (i.e. the collection of information from the external environment). The concept of information management and related concepts are explained and the differences between them identified. We present core definitions and theories and explore the constituent parts of information management as an organizational activity. In each case, we try to demonstrate the relevance of these activities to workplace information. Finally, we will draw some conclusions and propose a short bibliography for researchers.

Information management and the workplace

Information management can be viewed from different perspectives: those of information specialists, information system developers, business managers, human resource managers and employees. Each of these will have a slightly different view and use different terms for the same phenomena, or name the same things differently. Regardless of this, there is a common ground for information management in the workplace, be it a corporate, public or non-governmental organization. From the point of view of information in the workplace, we can identify two directions of research, one for 'corporate information management', and one for 'personal information management'.

Related to the concept of information management is a number of other concepts, which strive to identify what is managed in more precise or narrower terms. Records management, information resource management, information systems management, document and data management or similar concepts belong to this category. Others focus on the tools used in information management, such as information life cycle, information audit, environmental scanning, taxonomies, discovery systems or intranet. We are not going to give an exhaustive overview of these, but will outline the relevance of some of them to workplace information and we will illustrate some of these different concepts by the examples of Ann, Johan and Liila.

Ann, our cardiologist, will care most about the records of her patients. Following standard rules and using professional terminology, she will meticulously record her observations, such as pulse or temperature, and stories her patients tell, in the medical record. This record will include previous data about her patient recorded by other doctors: therapists, surgeons, ophthalmologists, etc., who have examined her patient over time, as well as test data coming from laboratories (blood tests, x-rays, tissue analysis, allergic reactions, etc.). These will be highly relevant when she makes prescriptions of medicine or other treatment. Since Ann works in Sweden, the file most likely will be only digital and will come from a large database holding records of many patients. In many countries, these digital records will be backed up by voluminous archives of paper records, one for each patient; thus, you may see nurses and clerks running around hospitals carrying these files from one room to another. Secure storage and accuracy of these records as well as their transfer between different medical institutions and doctors is of high importance, as any failure in this communication chain may result in the patient's death. Thus, medical record management is a focus in medical institutions, where the record itself is an information artefact of greatest importance for Ann to carry out her work (see Chapter 6).

Our lawyer Johan, a senior manager in the lawyers' firm, and his colleagues hire an assistant or a secretary who manages the paper documents, computer files, clients' records, court materials, juridical databases of court cases, legal codices and many other paper-based and digital information sources for the partners. This paralegal assistant may also have a duty to follow the news in the legal environment, such as changes in laws or new court cases coming up, and draw Johan's attention to them. She may also be in charge of digital tools used in the firm and help Johan to use those for finding or storing his materials. The firm will also have strict rules about confidential or private information relating to clients and cases, so Johan will need to be careful in locking up his papers in a safe or protecting computer files by passwords. All these intricate information resources will require careful management.

Liila, our journalist, will be most concerned with information novelty. She uses a lot of information sources, resources and processes for scanning her personal and corporate social networks by contacting various people in many ways each day. She searches for information using different internet tools, but also other media, such as radio or television, business bulletins or sports news on paper. She has developed a long tradition for tracking information through all possible channels and sources. If she is working on a 'hot' topic, she may be dealing with a huge number of digital files, as happened with the Panama papers.[1] The most important issue for her will be identifying the news value of information, even if it was produced long ago. Thus, sensitivity to the social environment and ability to locate information that will capture the attention of the widest (or targeted) public is instrumental in her workplace.

Our personae have different understandings of what is important in the information that they produce or use, but there is one common thing that can be visible in each of the examples: they are guided by the rules and demands of the professions that they belong to and the organizations they work for. These organizations create the criteria for assessing the value of information, but also offer various tools and procedures to work with it in the workplace.

Definition of information management

Information management is mainly understood as an area of practice and a part of organizational management. Information management as a practice refers to the actual improvement of the organizational environment, processes, tools and/or working conditions. Information management as part of organizational management strives for a better understanding or explanation of the role of information management in organizations, its functions and applications or the tasks and roles of information managers. In this chapter, we seek to explain the practical aspects of information management and the consequences to workplace information as it emerges in research literature. First, let us look at the definitions of information management.

Information management: its role in the organization and the workplace

We can distinguish three pre-computer-age areas that gave rise to information management. Black, Muddiman and Plant (2016) trace it back to the 19th-century office devices in industrial companies and governmental institutions, including military intelligence operations. Macevičiūtė and Wilson (2002) identify the concept of information as a resource emerging from the US Paperwork Reduction Act (Commission on Federal Paperwork, 1977). In both cases, information management is related to the emergence and development of modern bureaucracy. Rayward (1975), Buckland (2017) and Wright (2014) relate the start of information management (and information science, in general) to the proliferation of scholarly information and the efforts of Paul Otlet (1934) to create structures for its organization and dissemination. These concepts relate to the development of sciences and the multiplication of information sources.

Wilson (2003) defines information management as the field of activity in an organization and outlines a number of aspects and tools that may serve as a checklist of tasks for an information manager. According to his point of view:

> the scope of the field is taken to include: information requirements, the
> information life-cycle, information resources, the economics of information,
> tools such as information and communication audits and information
> mapping, information access, networks and intranets, legal aspects of access
> and privacy, information policy and strategy, and strategic information
> system.   (Wilson, 2003, 266–74)

Choo (2002) focuses on the main processes of information management, such as information acquisition, organization and use. He also suggests that these processes connect the management of information technologies, the management of information resources, information policies and standards, and information process (see Figure 4.1 on the next page). Each of them should be considered in relation to the others to bring the highest benefits for organizations.

In Figure 4.1 we see a synthesis of tools, processes and standards that also can be distinguished in each story of our persona.

Detlor links the processes of information management to efficiency and

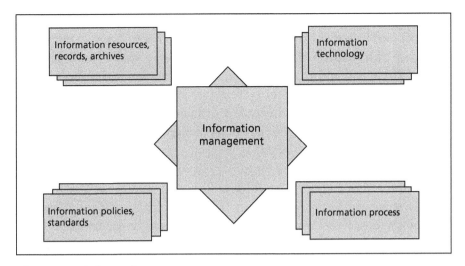

Figure 4.1 *Information management*

effectiveness, and as a result to increased competitive advantages of an organization, but also to the people performing working tasks in these organizations through increasing the awareness and competence of people. Thus, he tries to connect enterprise and personal information management:

> the management of the processes and systems that create, acquire, organize, store, distribute, and use of information. The goal of IM is to help people and organizations access, process and use information efficiently and effectively. Doing so helps organizations operate more competitively and strategically and helps people better accomplish their tasks and become better informed. (Detlor, 2010, 103)

We can see that each of these definitions unites various elements and parts of information management in an organization, but also keeps these elements separate. This shows the importance of each of them for organizations, and gives a more holistic picture of organizational information on a general level.

On the other hand, we also see that one of these elements – information technology – dominates large modern organizations. Examining the contents of the key journals in the field in 2004, Wilson and Macevičiūtė observed that organizational and human information management were discussed as part of managing information systems and information technology (Macevičiūtė and Wilson, 2005). The economic aspects, such as return on investment in information systems, led to the emergence of enterprise information management, information assets management (Ladley, 2010) and information governance. Information governance relates enterprise content management systems to the life cycle of records from their inception to deletion (Hullavarad, O'Hare and Roy, 2015, 261).

Thus, both enterprise information management and information governance emerged as functional areas in organizational information systems. The literature review shows very little overlap of these two terms with information needs in the workplace and mainly relates to the requirement for information systems. The literature is mainly focused on technology (e.g. cloud computing and data mining), business assets, risk management, data value chain, interaction and visualisation, and customisation of services for different devices.

Ann, Johan and Liila become users of these technologies which require training for using them. They may face a proliferation of information systems of various complexity that may be poorly adapted to their workplace requirements if the system developers do not take into account the differences of their professions and jobs.

The existing definitions of information management and neighbouring areas are derived from rather concrete practical processes of managing information in business and public organizations. The next section will include some theoretical concepts that explain the scope and extent of information management.

Theoretical underpinnings of information management

Recently, the attempt to create a more general conceptual framework of information management was undertaken by Madsen. She draws on the explorative investigations of information management research output by Schlögl (2005) and Macevičiūtė and Wilson (2005) and shows that most of the concepts related to information management are embedded in different disciplines. She identifies three notions of information management: 'Information Management 1' at institutional level, 'Information Management 2', which is content-oriented, and 'Information Management 3', rooted in information systems (Madsen, 2013, 535). According to her, these three concepts belong to two levels: the first one to the organizational and two others to the conceptual one, in which she identifies disciplines dealing with theoretical issues. The first one is important for us.

Though Madsen does not identify a discipline for the institutional level, a number of researchers apply approaches of organizational behaviour to information management. Choo has developed several models using this perspective based on the life cycle of information and organizational processes (Choo, 2002; 2006). In his earlier research Choo used to emphasise the benefits that information management brings to the competitive advantage and success of companies, but the starting point remained always with the information need of the people in the workplace. In his later studies, he also investigated the role of workers in creating effective information management tools (Choo et al., 2006). His integrated model (Choo, 2016, 144) includes different steps: identification, selection, acquisition, storing and modern storage spaces, processing, mining, dissemination, supply and deletion of information. In his latest book, Choo strengthens the component of personal behaviour and proposes a new model for integrating information-seeking and use behaviour with the information management cycle and processes. He develops a precise description of each process in relation to workplace information (Choo, 2016, 144). Thus, he brings together personal and organizational components, such as attitudes, assumptions and values held by organizational members about the role and place of information and social and physical settings of the organization, as mutually shaping each other and, especially, the information behaviour (Choo, 2016, 163). His model of organizational information behaviour also links his understanding of information management to the concept of information culture (see Chapter 2). It also argues that there are not only two main components within information management, namely, people shaping the organization and organizational features influencing people's behaviour, but also two potential aims of information management:

1 increasing organizational effectiveness and/or competitive advantage by improving internal and external processes, standards and tools
2 increasing employees' satisfaction with their work and the workplace by setting convenient and user-friendly routines, systems, procedures and improving the working environment by information management means.

These two goals do not need to be mutually exclusive, but in research we can identify two bodies of literature focusing on one or another.

Choo's understanding of information management is based on the information life cycle, a concept developed in records management. According to Wilson (2013), this life cycle includes three main parts: creation, information management and information use (Figure 4.2). While information management is dealing mainly with one part of the whole cycle, two other parts are of real concern for the workplace information and organizations, but neither of them can happen without the third part effectively. Information management staff, such as Johan's assistant, should be aware that creation and information use is their actual goal and be involved in governing these two processes as much as they can be governed.

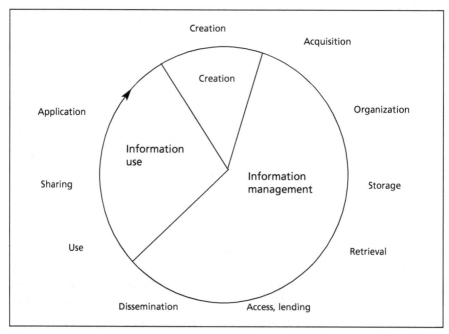

Figure 4.2 *Information life cycle* (source: Wilson, 2013)

The information life cycle lies in the foundation of most information management models and helps to identify the direction or movement of documents and data within the organization.

Related concepts

Personal information management

Studies of personal information management focus on the information behaviour of people in organizations. According to Jones and Teevan:

> Personal information management or PIM is both the practice and the study of the activities people perform to acquire, organize, maintain, retrieve, use, and control the distribution of information items such as documents (paper-based and digital), Web pages, and e-mail messages for everyday use to complete tasks (work-related and not) and to fulfil a person's various roles (as parent, employee, friend, member of community, etc.).
>
> (Jones and Teevan, 2007, 3)

Barreau (1995, 327) relates personal information management to the work environment and personal information seeking, organizing and use by employees who create special methods and rules for this purpose. Whittaker contrasts seeking for new information with 'personal information management where familiar information is used as a personal resource that we keep, manage, and (sometimes repeatedly) exploit' (Whittaker, 2011, 1). He calls this process personal information curation. According to him, people more often work with the information that they have already found and organize it for future use, rather than look for new information.

In her everyday work, our cardiologist Ann would more often turn to the shelves with her study textbooks and notes than search in MEDLINE databases for the newest clinical research. A search in MEDLINE is something she would do at some other time set aside for competence development or conference attendance. Our lawyer Johan may have the most important data on his clients' cases on the desktop of his computer organized in protected directories, while our journalist Liila may ransack the piles of papers on her desk because she remembers seeing something important among them two days ago.

Numerous studies about how much information people keep without deleting or throwing away provide support for this claim (e.g. Whittaker, Bellotti and Gwisdka, 2007). Researchers have studied how individuals organize paper material (Malone, 1983), photographs (Rodden and Wood, 2003), computer files (Khoo et al. 2007) or bookmarks (Aula, Jhaveri and Käki, 2005). The types and formats of materials define the methods and forms of keeping information as much as the aims for retaining it and the character of the individual. Bruce et al. (2011) conducted a study of how people keep and organize their information within long-term projects, observing the changes in methods of organization over time when people learn more about their own information needs and restructure their work. Other researchers have noticed that less structured keeping of information requires less resource and is usually related to more frequent use of the stored materials (Malone, 1983). Technology changes the habits for organizing materials, because it allows access to the stored files by navigating to them or searching, thus reducing the need for careful grouping and filing or remembering where they can be found.

According to Paganelli (2013), organizations set out to use common methods or common information strategies, but personal information activities are always specific. Therefore, Vacher (2004) has developed a notion of information bricolage. This suggests that in parallel with the strategies and systems provided by organizations, employees develop their own systems of search, storage and use of information. This helps them reduce the risk of information overload (Paganelli, 2013, 235–6). This was confirmed by investigating the personal information management of many different employees, for example, teachers (Diekema and Olsen, 2014) or engineers (Chaudhry and Al-Mahmud, 2015).

Recently researchers of personal information management produced four types of recommendations for information managers and tool developers that will help to solve many problems of information overload (Jones et al., 2015, 3516). They suggest taking into account the needs for:

1 information capture and retention for later use
2 finding and organizing information across applications
3 reminding and managing attention, tasks and to-dos
4 managing versions, controlling clutter and combatting fragmentation.

Information resource management

Information resource management as discussed by Wilson is synonymous with information management but refers to the information-holding entities that have relevance to the organizational goals and work tasks of employees. Thus, financial records are an important information resource for a company accountant, production data for a production manager and the addresses of customers for a salesman (Wilson, 1985, 63). These resources may be categorised according to the origin (internal and external), media (printed, digital, human), type (reports, statistical data, client records), or content (legal, technical, etc.). In addition, other people are important information resources for all employees in a company. Though information technology can also serve all if applied properly, our lawyer Johan may find a talk with his colleagues during an after-work visit to a pub more enlightening than a long search through the Lexis database.

Taylor (1982) speaks about the need for an organization to better integrate existing information by adding value to it through processing within information systems. However, it is the users who determine the value of information and they have to be taken into account when designing information systems. If our cardiologist Ann has to access crucial information about her patient through an incomprehensible interface and loses time when she needs to start an operation, she will not regard the system or information as valuable.

To understand the users, it is necessary to explore their environments from where the problems originate that require information in order to be solved (Taylor, 1982). Taylor talks more of an ideal user type in an ideal information use environment rather than of a personal employee. The concepts of the specific work environment and its elements are significant in relation to workplace information, as they take into account generic problems, solutions and accepted ways of applying them in different organizational and professional contexts (Taylor, 1991).

Byström's studies of the relation between work-task complexity and the required information sources and information types (Byström, 2002) are useful to further understand a workplace environment and the deployment of information resources within an organization so that the optimal information which is needed for a particular job task can be acquired. Her studies also point to the conditions that influence the choice to consult people as information sources. These findings add an additional aspect to workplace information that may focus not only on acquisition and organization, but also on dispensing and sharing information as a part of workplace information activities.

Some of the tools used in information management, such as enterprise information management systems, software, guidelines and specialised services, can help employees reduce the load of information handling. As we have already stated, however, they need to be helpful rather than increase the complexity of our workplace tasks. Thus, some old-time but constantly updated methods, such as information audits, are used to identify bottlenecks and problems.

Information audit

Information audit is a conceptual and practical tool that helps to align information work with the actual needs of an organization and people within it. Buchanan and Gibb define information audit as 'a holistic approach to identifying and evaluating an organization's information resources and information flow, in order to facilitate effective and efficient information systems' (Buchanan and Gibb, 2007, 171). They also explore existing methodologies (Buchanan and Gibb, 2008) and identify two main approaches: bottom-up, when information resources are discovered and mapped step by step, with each employee using them (as in Infomapping by Burk and Horton, 1988); and the top-down approach, placing more emphasis on the organizational analysis and information policy (as in Orna, 2008, or Henczel, 2001).

The first approach may be illustrated by information managers following our journalist Liila and noting what information sources she uses. They may discover that some of the expensive media databases are never used because they are badly designed, but boxes with old newspaper clippings are exploited intensively. Thus, new tasks are set for system designers to meet the need. The second approach may affect our cardiologist Ann when the hospital has to implement the new EU directive on data privacy and creates additional regulation for protection of medical records.

Information audits usually focus on internal information resources and flows, but they also can identify the channels of incoming information related to external information collection, or environmental scanning.

Strategic watch

The literature reflects how the area of information management has evolved over time. The importance of watching what is happening outside organizations was noticed quite early on. The concept of 'strategic watch' appeared in the 1960s, introduced by such researchers as Etzioni (1964) and Aguilar (1967), who explored the activities of scanning the business environment by modern organizations. They postulated that, to be effective, strategic management requires the consideration of the economic, social, political and technological dimensions of the external environment of the organization.

Lainee (1991) talked about the importance of a strategic technological watch. This means that the leader of the organization observes and acts upon developments pertaining to the commercial future of technologies and notes the technical capacities and choices of competitors. Lainee emphasised the necessity to watch narrow areas, in which crucial change is happening. Jakobiak and Dou defined the technological watch as the 'environmental observation and analysis followed by well-targeted dissemination of selected and processed information, useful for strategic decision-making' (Jakobiak and Dou, 1992). The technological watch is the 'bare or vital minimum' for organizations (Jakobiak, 2009, 31). Rouach (2010, 19–20) has proposed the concept of the pyramid of three main steps constituting the technical watch: at the bottom of it lies acquisition of information, the second step consists of transmission and storage of information and the final step includes synthesis of collected information for making strategic decisions. This is, in fact, a model of information management. However, he discovered that these methodical observations were too restrictive and a more global approach (economic intelligence) is required. This approach is closer to the strategic watch of Etzioni (1964) and Aguilar (1967). Nevertheless, the watch of specific parts of the organizational environment is still useful and depends on the nature and situation of an organization.

Competitive intelligence

Thus, commercial enterprises watch and analyse customers, suppliers and trends in the marketplace. They explore customers' satisfaction and follow the trends of their needs and demands in the future or explore the possibilities of new products and take into account the relations with suppliers. This concept has been referred to as 'competitive intelligence' by Porter in his two books on competitive strategy and competitive advantage (Porter, 1980; 1985). Competitive intelligence takes into account both current and future competitors. Martinet and Ribault (1988) postulate that competitive intelligence is important for all the departments of the enterprise and can work in synergy with other watches. According to Frion (2009), competitive intelligence literature mainly focuses on the organizational processes and does not take into account the research reported in information-behaviour research. Therefore, it does not explain the importance for competitive intelligence of employees' information collection and sharing.

Recently, many organizations have started following the development of human resources and observing closely the evolution of the workforce, the development of new training proposals, the changes in workplace environments and their costs in relation to the productivity achieved in a workplace (Belimane and Rhani, 2010, Chapter 2).

Martinet and Ribault tried to unite various 'watches' under the notion of industrial and global watch that takes into account social, cultural and political factors left out by other types of watch. At the end of the 20th century these authors were already talking about industrial scanning or environmental scanning, which requires a methodology to exploit effectively various sources of information and also a specific organization to exploit the synergy between various 'watches' in the company. Their concept is very close to 'environmental scanning' – the widest concept relating to collecting external information about all aspects of the environment in which organizations exist.

Environmental scanning

Environmental scanning is a natural feature of human beings and connects to our animal existence, when the surroundings had to be watched for potential danger or foraged for food. We all constantly look out for anything important for our survival or pleasure and for our studies or work. Our journalist Liila is so involved in her professional scanning of surroundings that she notices newsworthy events even when she is on holiday with her family or having fun with her friends. This is important to her work as a journalist that is directed to finding news. But any organization needs to collect and manage external information, as it helps to understand and explain the environment in which the organization exists and to adapt to it. For example, the lawyers' firm maintains the database of laws and regulations, in which our lawyer Johan registers any change that he has observed in his area of legal practice, but also searches for possible changes and interpretations registered by his colleagues. Thus, they ensure the quality and relevance of their legal service.

Environmental scanning is an important aspect of information management and decision making in organizations. According to Choo,

> Environmental Scanning is the acquisition and use of information about
> events, trends and relationships in an organization's external environment,
> the knowledge of which would assist management in planning the
> organization's future course of action.   (Choo, 2002, 227)

This activity constitutes a strategic mode of organizational learning and improves organizational performance.

All three of our personae will be involved in environmental scanning: Ann will be watching out for new operation methods and equipment, medicine and clinical research results by reading specialised journals and attending meetings; Johan will be looking for new clients, changes in laws and court regulations; not to speak of Liila, who earns her bread by her ability not only to watch out for new developments, but to be the first to notice and identify them.

In Figure 4.3, Choo has provided an integrated view of different types of environmental scanning, from those that involve short-term results and observe a narrow area of external environments, to the ones that can be used for long-term results and overview a broad picture of the societal environment.

The state-of-the-art study done by Choo (2002, 229) shows that environmental scanning should be planned and managed as a strategic activity and implemented as a formal system. It also underlines that users should participate actively throughout the scanning process, and information management should provide a firm foundation for the scanning system.

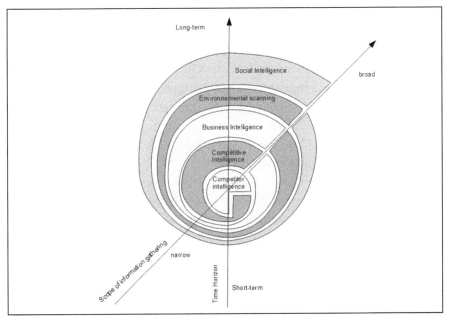

Figure 4.3 *Forms of organizational external information gathering* (based on Choo, 2002, 88)

Environmental scanning bridges organizational information management systems and personal information seeking in an organic way and pertains to seeking, organizing and using workplace information for particular organizational aims.

Conclusion: the future of information management and workplace information

The organizational approach to information management integrates the information science and information systems conceptual levels identified by Madsen (2013). It emphasises an organization as a collective information user and as a generator of an organizational information use environment. It also highlights an employee as the main agent not only of seeking internal and external information with the aims of the particular job and workplace in mind, but also as an active participant in the processes of information keeping, storing, organizing and reusing. All information user activities are constrained by rules, tools, values and conditions set by an organization. Information management is a tool to increase the success of an organization. All of these are, however, also influenced by requirements and the behaviour of employees, and the workplaces may change as a result. Workplace conditions and requirements are also changing under the influence of various factors in the environment.

It can be expected that future organizations will create extended actor networks of external and internal information resources and connect them with social networks of human beings in workplaces that would allow seamless transmission of information between the nodes, increase the benefits of information sharing and ensure effective use of content, data and even personal competence. One can even envision the artificial intelligence components used to increase the efficiency of connection management according to workplace needs and organizational decision making.

Information management connects with other concepts used in the investigation of workplace information and information in organizations, such as information overload, information products, information culture, information behaviour and others. It takes a managerial perspective that includes such aspects as ownership, costing and pricing of information resources, security, relevance to organizational goals, effectiveness of information use in decision making, reduction of equivocality and reduction of stress in the workplace.

The diversification of the activities, together with tools and procedures related to information work in organizations, affects the workplace and people in organizations, both positively and negatively. Consider such developments as mobile communication devices or social media, which, on the one hand, can ease information sharing but, on the other hand, intrude on the private time and life of employees. Seamless inclusion of the new tools and methods into the fabric of organizational information structures is one of the big tasks for the future of information management.

As information systems management dominates in modern organizations, the future of information management relates not so much to the performance of these systems as to their suitability for the purposes of organizations and employees. Connecting personal and organizational requirements and implementing them in user-friendly applications might be one of the major challenges of future information management.

Note

1 The Panama papers relate to a scandal caused in 2016 by the leaking of 11.5 million documents detailing financial and attorney–client information for more than 214,488 offshore entities and concern a number of politicians and celebrities around the world.

References

Aguilar, F. J. (1967) *Scanning the Business Environment*, Macmillan.

Aula, A., Jhaveri, N. and Käki, M. (2005) Information Search and Re-access Strategies of Experienced Web Users. In Ellis, A. and Hagino, T. (eds), *Proceedings of the 14th International World Wide Web Conference WWW'05*, ACM, 583–92.

Barreau, D. K. (1995) Context as a Factor in Personal Information Management Systems, *Journal of the American Society for Information Science*, **46** (5), 327–39.

Belimane, W. and Rhani, A. (2010) *La Mise en Place d'un Système de Veille Commerciale*, Alger, EHEC ex INC.

Black, A., Muddiman, D. and Plant, H. (2016) *The Early Information Society: information management in Britain before the computer*, Routledge.

Bruce, H., Wenning, A., Jones, E., Vinson, J. and Jones, W. (2011) Seeking an Ideal Solution to the Management of Personal Information Collections,

Information Research, **16** (1), paper 462, http://InformationR.net/ir/16-1/paper462.html.

Buchanan, S. and Gibb, F. (2007) Information Audit: role and scope, *International Journal of Information Management*, **27** (3), 159–72.

Buchanan, S. and Gibb, F. (2008) Information Audit: methodology selection, *International Journal of Information Management*, **28** (1), 1–33.

Buckland, M. (2017) *Paul Otlet: pioneer of information management*, http://people.ischool.berkeley.edu/~buckland/otlet.html.

Burk, C. F. and Horton, F. W. (1988) *InfoMap: a complete guide to discovering corporate information resources*, Prentice-Hall.

Byström, K. (2002) Information and Information Sources in Tasks of Varying Complexity, *Journal of the Association for Information Science and Technology*, **53** (7), 581–91.

Chaudhry, A. S. and Al-Mahmud, S. (2015) Information Literacy at Work: a study on information management behaviour of Kuwaiti engineers, *The Electronic Library*, **33** (4), 760–72.

Choo, C. W. (2002) *Information Management for the Intelligent Organization*, 3rd edn, Information Today.

Choo, C. W. (2006) *The Knowing Organization: how organizations use information to construct meaning, create knowledge, and make decisions*, Oxford University Press.

Choo, C. W. (2016) *The Inquiring Organization: how organizations acquire knowledge and seek information*, Oxford University Press.

Choo, C. W., Furness, C., Paquette, S., van den Berg, H., Detlor, B., Bergeron, P. and Heaton, L. (2006) Working with Information: information management and culture in a professional services organization, *Journal of Information Science*, **32** (6), 491–510.

Commission on Federal Paperwork (1977) *Information Resources Management*, US Government Printing Office.

Detlor, B. (2010) Information Management, *International Journal of Information Management*, **30** (2), 103–8.

Diekema, A. R. and Olsen, M. W. (2014) Teacher Personal Information Management (PIM), Practices: finding, keeping, and re-finding information, *Journal of the Association for Information Science and Technology*, **65** (11), 2261–77.

Etzioni, A. (1964) *Modern Organizations*, Prentice-Hall.

Frion, P. (2009) What Information Behaviour Can Offer to Competitive Intelligence, *International Symposium Models, Methods, Engineering of*

Competitive intelligence, Beaulieu-sur-Mer, 25–26 November, http://www.acrie.fr.

Frost, R. B. and Choo, C. W. (2017) Revisiting the Information Audit: a systematic literature review and synthesis, *International Journal of Information Management*, **37** (1–A), 1380–90, www.sciencedirect.com/science/article/pii/S0268401216303243?via%3Dihub.

Henczel, S. (2001) *The Information Audit: a practical guide*, K. G. Saur.

Hullavarad, S., O'Hare, R. and Roy, A. K. (2015) Enterprise Content Management Solutions: roadmap strategy and implementation challenges, *International Journal of Information Management*, **35** (2), 260–5.

Jakobiak, F. and Dou, H. (1992) De l'Information Documentaire à la Veille Technologique pour l'Entreprise, Enjeux, Aspects Généraux et Définitions. In Desvals H. and Dou, H. (eds) *La Veille Technologique, l'Information Scientifique, Technique et Industrielle*, Dunod, 2–45.

Jakobiak, F. (2009) *L'Intelligence Économique, Techniques et Outils*, 2nd edn, Eyrolles.

Jones, W. (2012) *The Future of Personal Information Management, Part I: our information, always and forever* (Synthesis lectures on information concepts, retrieval, and services), Morgan & Claypool.

Jones, W. P. and Teevan, J. (2007) *Personal Information Management*, University of Washington Press.

Jones, W. P., Capra, R., Diekema, A., Teevan, J., Pérez-Quiñones, M., Dinnean, J. D. and Hemminger, B. (2015) 'For Telling' the Present: using the Delphi method to understand personal information management practices. In Begole, B. and Kim, J. (eds) *Proceedings of the 33rd Annual ACM Conference on Human Factors in Computing Systems CHI'15*, ACM, 3513–22.

Khoo, C., Luyt, B., Ee, C., Osman, J., Lim, H. H. and Yong, S. (2007) How Users Organize Electronic Files on their Workstations in the Office Environment: a preliminary study of personal information organization behaviour, *Information Research*, **12** (2), paper 293 http://InformationR.net/ir/12-2/paper293.html.

Ladley, J. (2010) *Making Enterprise Information Management (EIM) Work for Business: a guide to understanding information as an asset*, Elsevier.

Lainee, F. (1991) *La Veille Technologique*, Eyrolles.

Macevičiūtė, E. and Wilson, T. D. (2002) The Development of the Information Management Research Area, *Information Research*, **7** (3), http://InformationR.net/ir/7-3/paper133.html.

Macevičiūtė, E. and Wilson, T. D. (2005) The Development of the Information Management Research Area. In Macevičiūtė, E. and Wilson, T. D. (eds), *Introducing Information Management: an information research reader*, Facet Publishing, 18–30.

Madsen, D. (2013) Disciplinary Perspectives on Information Management, *Procedia – Social and Behavioral Sciences*, **73**, 534–7.

Malone, T. W. (1983) How do People Organize their Desks: implications for the design of office information systems, *ACM Transactions on Office Information Systems*, **1** (1), 99–112.

Martinet, B. and Ribault, J.-M. (1988) *La Veille Technologique, Concurrentielle et Commerciale*, Les Éditions d'Organization.

Orna, E. (2008) Information Policies: yesterday, today, tomorrow, *Journal of Information Science*, **34** (4), 547–66.

Otlet, P. (1934) *Traité de Documentation: le livre sur le livre, théorie et pratique*, Brussels, Eds Mundaneum.

Paganelli, C. (2013) *Une Approche Info-communicationnelle des Activités Informationnelles en Contexte de Travail: acteurs, pratiques et logiques sociales*, Sciences de l'information et de la communication, Université de Grenoble, https://tel.archives-ouvertes.fr/tel-00776667/document.

Porter, M. E. (1980) *Competitive Strategy: techniques for analysing industries and competitors*, Free Press.

Porter, M. E. (1985) *The Competitive Advantage: creating and sustaining superior performance*, Free Press.

Rayward, W. B. (1975) The Universe of Information : the work of Paul Otlet for documentation and international organization, All-Union Institute for Scientific and Technical Information (VINITI).

Rodden, K. and Wood, K. R. (2003) How do People Manage their Digital Photographs? In Cockton, G. and Korhonen, P. (eds), *Proceedings of the SIGCHI Conference on Human Factors in Computing Systems ChI'03*, ACM, 409–16.

Rouach, D. (2010) *La Veille Technologique et l'Intelligence Économique*, 5th edn, Presses Universitaires de France.

Schlögl, C. (2005) Information and Knowledge Management: dimensions and approaches, *Information Research*, **10** (4), paper 235, http://InformationR.net/ir/10-4/paper235.html.

Taylor, R. S. (1982) Value-added Processes in the Information Life Cycle, *Journal of the Association for Information Science and Technology*, **33** (5), 341–6.

Taylor, R. S. (1991) Information Use Environments. In Dervin, B. (ed.), *Progress in Communication Sciences*, Vol. 10, Ablex, 217–25.

Vacher, B. (2004) Du Bricolage Informationnel á la Litote Organizationnelle: ou comment considérer le bricolage au niveau stratégique?, *Revue Sciences de la Société*, **63** – *Systèmes d'information organizationnels?*, 133–50.

Whittaker, S. (2011) Personal Information Management: from information consumption to curation, *Annual Review of Information Science and Technology (ARIST)*, **45**, 1–42.

Whittaker, S., Bellotti, V., and Gwisdka, J. (2007) Everything Through E-mail. In Jones, W. and Teevan, J. (eds), *Personal Information Management*, University of Washington Press, 167–89.

Wilson, T. D. (1985) Information Management, *The Electronic Library*, **3** (1), 62–6.

Wilson, T. D. (2003) Information Management. In Feather, J. and Sturges, P. (eds), *International Encyclopedia of Information and Library Science*, Routledge, 263–78.

Wilson, T. D. (2013) *Information Management*, Citisendium, http://en.citisendium.org/wiki/Information_management.

Wright, A. (2014) *Cataloguing the World: Paul Otlet and the birth of the information age*, Oxford University Press.

5

Information artefacts

Katriina Byström and Nils Pharo

Introduction

In today's society, information artefacts are omnipresent. In this chapter, we introduce them as part of a conceptual framework for workplace information, and, accordingly, within the scope of information science. We analyse them from three theoretical underpinnings: materiality, plasticity and context. Information artefacts are outlined as *information sources* and *information channels* from the perspective of workers. Information sources are commonly understood as carriers of information and knowledge, and information channels as means of connecting to those sources. In addition, we present three categories of *information tools*: tools for storage, for collaboration and for retrieval and searching, and make a closer examination of the concepts of *information systems, social media* and *enterprise information search*. The artefacts' agency in the context of work is illustrated through three central information-related activities: information seeking, information searching and information needs. We conclude by addressing two new areas of future research and development concerning information artefacts at workplaces: collegial inclusion and forms of expertise.

In our case, the objects of interest are those that deal with information or knowledge, either by encompassing information and knowledge, providing access to them, or facilitating the production of them. It is tempting to provide a seemingly simple example, such as a book or a search engine, but as the chapter will illustrate, information artefacts are complex phenomena that do not neatly organize themselves into straightforward categories or hierarchies. The conceptualisation of information artefacts acknowledges their agency in information interactions as well as their contextual transformations. This makes them different from the other, but related, concept of information objects that are viewed as more static, storable and findable items (cf. Chapter 6, 'Information attributes'). We perform this conceptual analysis of information artefacts in the area of workplace information: that is, with a focus on information and knowledge in instances of work, and as part of the interdisciplinary field of information science.

During nearly all of our waking time we interact with some kind of information artefacts. Let us take as an example Ann, who is a cardiologist in a large city hospital. In the mornings when Ann wakes up early, she listens to *the morning news on the radio*, if she has more time she prefers to read *the newspaper* whilst having breakfast. On her way out, she checks *the bus timetable* on her phone, and while on the bus, she glimpses through *her feeds in Facebook and Instagram*, and reads the most interesting *Tweets*. If the traffic is slow, she even might check *her e-mail*; if not, she does this at the very latest whilst settling down at her office with a cup of coffee. When picking up this drink in a coffee bar located in the hospital entrance hall, she had a quick chat with a couple of *her peers*. She learned that the ongoing renovation in the reception area would take longer than planned, and reflected upon the difficulties that some of her patients had been complaining about. They had found it difficult to find their way in the labyrinth of temporarily arranged passages with confusing *signs with an arrow* pointing into a specific direction and then disappearing when arriving at the next junction of passages. 'Well, well, not much to do about it', Ann sighs, as she reads a confirmation about the delay on *the hospital intranet*. After attending to *her e-mails* and finishing the coffee, she turns her attention to *her calendar* for appointments and to *the medical record* of her first patient scheduled for an appointment at nine o'clock. She glimpses through *the shared notes in the record* and *a personal, informal one* reminding her that the patient was to become a grandfather after their last meeting. She notes that a part of the result for a previously ordered *laboratory test* is missing in *the record* and she phones the lab to request the missing value. *The laboratory assistant* reviews *the lab register of test results*, finds the missing part and provides the result to Ann, as he simultaneously updates *the electronic patient record*. *The complementary result* causes Ann to reconsider the patient's medication, and after consulting *the drug database*, she even phones *a colleague* in order to check her reasoning and together they probe *the Medline database* for the most current scientific recommendation. At exactly on the hour, Ann opens the door and asks the receptionist nurse to guide the patient to her office. After greeting the patient and asking about the birth of the grandchild, Ann turns to the medical issue at hand and *asks the patient* how he feels, if he considers his condition better or worse, if he has been feeling nausea or pain. So, by just a couple of minutes past nine in the morning, Ann has been in contact with some 20 information artefacts, probably more. Those with immediate interest for her work are her e-mail, her colleague, her patient, the intranet, her calendar, a medical record, a personal note, a laboratory test, laboratory assistant and a medical database.

Information artefacts come in many formats; for instance, digitised, in print, as broadcasts, as databases, as registers, as persons, as signposts, as timetables, as social media platforms, as news, as laboratory tests, as records, etc. Moreover, they may be formal and informal, as well as internal or external to the work organization, and chosen for use on the basis of personal preferences and expectations as well as socio-cultural practices formed in the workplace. Next, we will scrutinise the theoretical underpinnings related to information artefacts to understand them in the context of work.

Theoretical underpinnings for information artefacts

In this section, we briefly discuss different perspectives open to understand the prerequisites of information artefacts. Even if, in most cases, it may seem self-evident that information artefacts have a physical material form, the nature of this and its relationship to information-related activities – such as information seeking, information searching, information need, among others – has largely been neglected (Pilerot, 2014). More recently, this has gained attention in information science through use of concepts such as socio-materiality. Orlikowski (2010) was among the first to address how material and social dimensions interact in work organizational settings. In a similar vein, we argue that the physical material form is only partial and needs to be complemented with intangible aspects of information artefacts in order to gain a comprehensive understanding of them in information science (cf. McKenzie, 2015; Orlikowski and Yates, 1994).

In the present chapter we do not provide a discussion of what is information or not, or what is knowledge and what is not. Neither will we make a distinction between information and knowledge. We simply settle for stating that information artefacts are objects that deal with information and knowledge. Whereas we will consistently use the term information artefact, we use interchangeably the terms 'information' and 'knowledge' when referring to the content that the artefacts deal with. We conclude with the view that information artefacts have (im)materiality that influences the user either as tangible physical objects, such as a hammer or a tractor, or as intangible objects lacking a physical form, for example signs, symbols or language, that become represented within designs, classifications or computer programmes. We define information artefacts simply as means that mediate information work; a definition that acknowledges both material and non-material formats and the relationship between the two.

In addition to the aspect of (im)materiality, another important aspect is the purpose of the artefacts. Information artefacts can be either originally created to deal with information, or despite the original aim come to be used for this purpose. Thus, we acknowledge the significance of human agency in reconfiguring and reconstructing an artefact in practice, the 'plasticity' of artefacts *per se* and their proximity to the context of use. Moreover, we also include into the notion of information artefacts entities that stretch the view of 'being man-made'. Whereas an information system or a book easily falls into the definition, a colleague or a medical doctor requires a closer explanation. A person's expressed knowledge may be referred to as an information artefact, when it is their socially and culturally constructed knowledge that is in focus. Ann, who is an established cardiologist, may thus be seen as a trained practitioner of modern cardiovascular medical practice, in instances where knowledge of heart diseases is expressed. Medicine is a 'man-made' trade, and Ann's training builds on the knowledge and beliefs held by the profession (cf. Taylor, 1991; Berg and Bowker, 1997). Huvila (2013) notes that work in the context of a museum is supported both by documents, information systems and physical collections of artefacts, but also by routines and internalised knowledge, similar to the knowledge held by Ann. Returning to the plasticity of information artefacts, together with their proximity to context, we can develop our reasoning: Ann was, in the above example, constructed as an information artefact based on her expertise in medicine. However, if she were to suffer a heart attack and become a patient, she would then be reconstructed as an information artefact based on her medical condition. Outside the present scope of information science and workplace information, or outside the medical setting, Ann naturally exists as something other than an information artefact of one kind or another.

Even though we adopt theoretically such a wide vantage point, our approach is more limited as to the selection of specific concepts to be discussed in the chapter. The aim is to provide a conceptual base for understanding and researching information artefacts in the workplace. Accordingly, we strive to keep the concepts on a broad enough level to offer a foundation for linking the more specific objects of study or development into a general terminology within the workplace information framework. This provides freedom for choosing a topic of one's own interest, but at the same time offers the possibility to aggregate the findings into a general theme of interest in the field of workplace information.

Key concepts: information source and information channel

Perhaps the most used and studied aspect of information artefacts in information science is through their conceptualisation as *information sources* from the perspective of workers. Information sources can range from literature, to colleagues, to project documentation and to events or observed objects. Early on, a set of information sources was identified in work environments: handbooks, procedures, memoranda, a newsletter, a unit supervisor, other team members, clients, other workers outside the team or unit, training sessions and other sources outside the team or unit – often collated into documentary sources and people as information sources (e.g. O'Reilly, 1982). The scope of identified information sources mirrors the professions that gained the most attention in the early research studies: scientists and engineers. Despite the traditionally heavy emphasis placed on sources of recorded information in information science, both individual people – especially peers but also other people involved in various roles – as well as groups or networks of people have been recognised as an important category of information sources in the work context (e.g. Paisley, 1968; Widén-Wulff, 2007; Hertzum, 2014).

Allen (1969) introduced the concept of gatekeepers to information science, who both gained and distributed valuable information through their networks. Later on, even events and physical objects observed were included as potential information sources at work. Byström and Järvelin

(1995), and with greater emphasis Veinot (2007), recognised visual cues as an additional type of information source. Lloyd (2006) concluded that information captured in the different types of sources was also of different kinds, as textual, social or physical. Thus, information sources may refer to both the kind of artefact *and* the kind of information mediated. One might argue that sources for physical information, like a fire or a piece of landscape, can hardly be described as 'man-made'. However, as in the case of patients' bodies turning into medical objects through the 'reading' by medical doctors like Ann, our cardiologist, so can a fire be read by a firefighter (cf. Lloyd, 2006) or a piece of landscape by a landscape architect. Similarly, a juridical event, whose very existence rests on shared social construction, such as a court meeting, may 'be read' differently by Liila, our journalist, and Johan, our lawyer. Berg and Bowker (1997) cite the case of patients' bodies turning into medical bodies, emphasising the focus on medical aspects of bodies from the perspective of medically trained professionals. Such reconfiguration of a body includes, in addition to the focus on the treatment of the disorder, also a focus on the treatment trajectory that places the body in a timescale of caregivers, rather than that of the patient (cf. Davies and McKenzie, 2004). Information may thus be available in printed, oral, digital and diverse corporeal formats; memos, colleagues, e-mails and images are common examples in workplace settings, but so also are human expressions such as a sudden cry of pain or material objects such as a sample of blood. For a medical doctor, all of the above may function as sources of information.

As the above discussion indicates, the concept of information source invites a variety of views and interpretations as a carrier of required, wanted or otherwise interesting and relevant information for work. It also invites criticism, for instance due to the often pseudo-neutral and straightforward one-sided connotations related to the definitions. As with many other activities in the workplace, the use of information and its sources as well as their associated strategies and goals is also guided by formal and informal social norms and by conventions of the workplace (cf. Salancik and Pfeffer, 1978; Giddens, 1984; cf. Chapter 3 above, 'Information culture'). In most workplaces, the most conventional information sources are made readily available in order to make work flow efficiently. At the same time, workers come to prioritise some knowledge over others. Furthermore, they become part of the activities learned in relation to general and local work practices. For instance, Ann has been guided to use certain information sources during her education and training to become an accredited physician (a professional practice; e.g. Taylor, 1991) as well as a practising physician at the hospital where she works (a local practice; e.g. Wenger-Trayner and Wenger-Trayner, 2014). Other participants, as well as the material and intellectual objects of the practice, including information sources, carry with them traditions, values and an agreed-upon set of facts that form the specific work context. Taylor (1991) referred to information use environments where people, problems, their resolutions and the accentuated contextual aspects together form premises for information use. These constitute an information use environment that both guides and places expectations on which information sources to use. Thus, there is a push in any work practice to look for certain information, to get hold of it through certain ways and to utilise certain information from certain sources. Brown and Duguid (2017) discuss the social life of information, and one may easily extend the discussion to apply also to the sources of information as an inseparable part of information sharing.

However, such socio-material or socio-cognitive structures are not fixed in isolation or demarcated to people's actions. People are able to choose not to comply with an existing practice, which may or may not lead to changes in the practice (e.g. Giddens, 1984; Billet, 2004; Wenger-Trayner and Wenger-Trayner, 2014). The use of information sources is one such work practice affected by social norms and individual aims. Nordsteien and Byström (2018) demonstrate how newly accredited nurses make an effort to change the patterns of information-source use in their workplace. As a participant in the workplace activities, a person assumes not only a role of an able worker in her setting, but also that of an active participant in the practice(s) involved; mediating, changing and thus developing the traditions, values and facts further, among relevant information and relevant information sources.

A related concept to information source is *information channel*, which refers to the medium used to access information sources. Sometimes it refers broadly to all kinds of intermediaries between a person looking for information and the information sought (e.g. Byström and Järvelin, 1995), and other times it is related to communication media, which place emphasis on material aids to access information sources (e.g. Daft and Lengel, 1996; Jung and Lyytinen, 2014). Examples of the first kind are librarians, information search engines and peers who know whom to turn to, whereas using a mobile phone to get hold of a colleague or to access a database, or communicating through a chat or wiki are examples of the latter understanding of an information channel. In the literature, information sources and information channels are sometimes used interchangeably, not only because of a careless use of the concepts but also due to the changing function of these information artefacts. For example, whereas Ann, our cardiologist, often is able to provide an answer to questions within her area of expertise, i.e. acting as an information source, occasionally she may not know the answer or only be able to answer a part of the question. In such cases, she guides the requester to another colleague for further information, and thus Ann functions as an information channel. Similarly, a web search engine can function as either an information source or an information channel. If Ann's patient enters query terms 'cardiogenic shock' in a modern internet search engine, at the top of the results page the search engine will return a 'featured snippet', i.e. a text box synthesising and summarising the condition and its cause. If the information provided proves relevant to the patient, the search engine has functioned as an information source from the perspective of the patient; that is, by collapsing several steps into one it has provided the information looked for. In other cases – or for less advanced search engines – and for queries where more complicated knowledge is targeted, additional steps need to be taken. For example, the query 'percutaneous coronary intervention', which refers to a non-surgical procedure to improve the blood flow to the heart, might return a list of results from which the searcher must choose to click on the links that seem to lead to relevant resources that actually access the information sought for. Thus the search engine, in this case, functions as an information channel, whereas the resources linked to are potential information sources.

Use of information sources and channels

Research on the use of information sources (and channels) at work is a central topic within the research field of information behaviour (e.g. Case and Given, 2016). The research field of interactive information retrieval focuses primarily on the interaction between users and digital information systems (e.g. Ruthven, 2008; Kelly, 2009). This is often called 'information searching' and describes a user's employment of an information retrieval system for the satisfaction of an information need (e.g. Wilson, 1999). 'Information seeking' (e.g. Wilson, 1999) denotes research on the use of information sources and channels in general to find information in order to perform a task or solve a problem. Byström and Hansen (2005) have developed a framework where information seeking and information searching are related in a comprehensive manner to facilitate research within the workplace information field. In the context of work, a work task is one node where several informational aspects play together. Work tasks are not owned by the context where they take place or the person performing the tasks; instead, they are mutually negotiated instances of work where personal preferences, professional principles and organizational accountability all influence their construction and performance. As Ann meets her patient, her individual beliefs, her professional ethics and the expectations of her colleagues and patients all guide her decisions about how to perform the task of diagnosing and treating the patient. Within this amalgamated context she decides what information needs to be acquired in addition to what she already knows, what sources and channels are reasonable to use, what information is likely to be found from which sources, what channels could be necessary to turn to and what are her expectations of information to be found. For the selection of information channels and sources, Zipf's principle of least effort, as either easy access or low costs to reach a good enough result, has been found to be an influential aspect in many studies over a long period (e.g. Hardy, 1982; Chang, 2016). This has, however, been contested in certain work situations. For instance, a review of research on choosing expert sources confirmed that quality is an important aspect alongside accessibility (Hertzum, 2014).

Whereas information seeking consists of the above activities related to information sources and channels alongside the evaluative phase of the information acquired from the different sources, Byström and Hansen (2005) separate information searching as concerning the interaction with a specific source or channel to retrieve information sought after. These interactions may, as is commonly referred to, focus on digital information resources. Stenmark (2010) found that despite heavy reliance on search engines outside work, many choose to navigate through menus at work, with poor and time-consuming results. Teevan et al. (2004) identified this as a kind of 'stepping behaviour' that builds on employees' contextual knowledge and is preferred over the use of keywords to directly target the sought information, even when they know what they were looking for. Whether this kind of trailing strategy holds also in relation to use of other information channels and sources is an open question. Pharo and Järvelin (2006) point out that information searching may often seem 'irrational', since the searchers tend to favour satisficing and incremental search strategies, as compared to the way textbooks on searching prescribe optimising query formulation (identify need, choose keywords, including synonyms, identify appropriate features available in the search engine – such as Boolean operators, enter query, evaluate and, if necessary reformulate query). This may be explained by the expectations from their work environment (cf. Taylor, 1991) or their (lack of) training in information literacy. Smith and Kantor (2008) have shown, however, that users invest extra effort to get the most out of poor search systems. Personal characteristics such as tenacity and stamina, and knowledge of specific terminology within one's work field, may thus compensate for challenges created by bad system usability or efficiency.

Byström and Hansen (2005) do not differentiate between different kinds of resources in defining information seeking versus searching. They choose instead to emphasise the scope of the activity. In this perspective, information searching is seen to concentrate on finding a specific piece of information from a specific source, whereas information seeking is understood to have the larger scope of all informational requirements for a work task, or a separable part of it. Sometimes a work task requires combined use of several information resources, sometimes it can be resolved by using one single source; in the latter case, information-seeking activity is redundant. For Ann these theoretical conceptualisations are probably irrelevant but in research on workplace information they facilitate understanding the phenomena. When diagnosing a patient's condition, Ann examines the patient and asks him questions, she consults his medical record; in addition she may ask a colleague about an unusual symptom, and perform a query in the Medline database. In Byström and Hansen's terms, all these would be instances of searching with different informational goals. Ann would not expect to get the same information from her patient as from her colleague, nor would she formulate her requests in a similar manner. Ann might also choose to consult both her colleague and the Medline database in pursuit of the same information; if the first used provides the desired information, the other would probably not be used. Should both of them be used, her interaction with the two would hardly be similar. As the separate consultations with the chosen sources are brought together, they form the activity of information seeking in order to diagnose the condition.

Key concept: information tool

Above, we made a fleeting reference to information channels viewed as communication channels, which is a definition less often addressed in information science. However, it relates to an umbrella concept of an *information tool*, which is seldom used as such in the research literature but of particular importance for information science. It captures the tacit understanding of the main aspect of interest of the more general and more generally utilised concept of information and communication technology (ICT): that is, the use and usefulness of ICT in different work contexts (cf. Zmud, 1983; Treem and Leonardi, 2013; Jarrahi and Thomson, 2017; Forsgren and Byström, 2018). With this concept we refer to tools that support core information practices at the workplace: for example, searching for and seeking information, information sharing and collaboration. Much research is concentrating on finding recorded information, such as documentation of projects or decisions (e.g. Gordon, 1997). Although finding expertise has always been of interest, the changes in organizational structures and work patterns have made it a hot research topic from the perspective of organizations' knowledge management. Leonardi (2015) found that enterprise social media increase employees' ambient awareness, in the sense that they mediate subtle cues about who knows what and who knows whom in the workplace. Hertzum (2014) reviews research in this area and arrives at the conclusion that knowledgeable colleagues in the work group or otherwise personally connected to it are the sources most often relied upon for information, and increasingly so as the work tasks become more challenging (e.g. Byström and Järvelin, 1995). His conclusion strengthens the long-lasting conclusion from the 1960s that the colleague is the most useful source at the workplace (cf. Allen, 1969). So far, digital development and the information practices of the born-digital generation have not changed this. People's capacity to both elaborate a topic and cope with uncertainty continues to be seen as the main reason for their primacy over other types of sources (Hertzum, 2014).

Finally, an employee may draw upon a variety of tools for storing and retrieving information. These tools range from organizational repositories for digital documents to physical documents on bookshelves. Jones (2007) has identified different strategies for personal information management (PIM), such as 'piling' and 'filing', for information in both physical and digital formats. Tools used for collaboration include for example e-mail or chat messaging and digital meetings that influence processes such as information sharing. Forsgren and Byström (2018) found that social media brought coherence in distributed work activities in a flat, agile workplace; a finding relating to Davies and McKenzie's (2004) conclusion about a 'prompt book' that co-ordinates temporal diversity among participating professionals in preparation for a theatre play, much in a similar manner that antenatal records function at a midwifery clinic. At workplaces, both new and old tools are utilised for information sharing and collaboration, as well as both physical (e.g. whiteboards and Post-It notes) and digital (e.g. e-mail and enterprise social media), which raises dilemmas in relation to the use of new tools for organizational communication (with clients, suppliers and others) within and outside the organization (e.g. Forsgren and Byström, 2018). Jarrahi and Thompson (2017) studied how mobile knowledge workers handle their informational requirements, as they lack a physical workplace. They found that the workers developed a number of secondary practices to secure their access to both social and factual information required to perform their core work tasks. These practices stretched from simply securing an electrical power supply and internet connection or having files available offline, to finding ways to maintain social ties to their colleagues.

Key concept: information system

Changing from the perspective of workers to that of work organizations, it is an *information system* that is the recurrent referential that relates to nearly all of the above concepts. The term is used in very different ways in the literature across many fields, as an organizing mechanism or as a synonym for a collection of technological information artefacts. However, a more significant common denominator is the organized nature of the contents for a purpose of handling information. Thus, an information system might equally well refer to the work organization itself as to a software program used for e.g. filling in and issuing travel reimbursements. As an information artefact in the field of information science and workplace information, information systems lay emphasis on the latter understanding: a tool for governing, systematising and managing information.

A company intranet is a particular kind of information channel and source as well as an information-sharing tool; through the structure of the intranet, a lot of information is made available. For instance, a website on the intranet by the human resources department about how to apply for travel reimbursement with a link to an application system for filling in data about travel costs is an example of an intranet being at the same time an information channel, source and sharing tool. The intranet is a service through which information, information sources and additional information channels are accessible. To retrieve the information stored in the system it must be indexed. Indexing can be in the form of manual or semi-automatic assignment of metadata (Lancaster, 2003) or be based on algorithms for automatic indexing (Baeza-Yates and Ribeiro-Neto, 2011). Whereas manual indexing is based on the indexer's topic knowledge and indexing expertise, automatic indexing makes use of statistical term distribution and linguistic theory to determine how to best represent the document's content. The appropriate indexing and retrieval methods must be based on the type of information stored in the system and the types of information needs that the system is expected to serve. For a system that manages large amounts of unstructured information, such as the world wide web, automatic indexing of the full text is today viewed as the best option. In a subject-specific database, on the other hand, it is common to use a controlled vocabulary, such as a thesaurus, to index the content. Such databases often do not contain the full text of the documents and thus using a controlled vocabulary makes it possible to secure consistency in indexing. Medical doctors, such as Ann, must rely on Medline and other databases being consistently indexed, therefore research into Medline indexing consistency is common (see e.g. Wilczynski and Haynes, 2009).

Data storage tools have increasingly evolved into tools for collaboration. Cloud storage provides data storage on centrally organized servers, which makes the data accessible from anywhere. Facilities for collaboration, e.g. in the form of real-time co-writing, which was an idea already explored in the 1960s, but which gained speed with the evolution of the web (Noël and Robert, 2002) and even more with the 'social web' of the mid-2000s, has dramatically changed the possibilities for working. If the hospital where Ann works implements such a solution, Ann can do parts of her work from home or while travelling. Some cloud services also facilitate the possibility of co-documentation and data sharing. She may meet her patients in a digital environment and during the counselling access the relevant medical files and laboratory results for reading and revising in a same manner as from her office at the hospital. Even her patients may access documentation made digitally available for them (cf. Huvila et al., 2018). It also provides Ann, who is involved in an international research project in cardiology, with an opportunity to use a document-sharing service when co-authoring scientific articles with her colleagues at other institutions around the world. In addition to opening new opportunities to interact with her patients and her colleagues over distance, she may find cloud services useful even in collaborations with colleagues at the same hospital, e.g. for writing procedure descriptions or having a digital meeting with a busy colleague at the opposite end of the hospital. However, these new opportunities are not without controversies, mostly due to security, long-time preservation and the dominance of commercial vendors among cloud service providers. Among others, Lindh and Nolin (2016) are concerned about the privacy issues and concealed immaterial costs of utilising commercial service providers for handling information. Even if the commercial service providers do not distribute the data stored and managed through their services as such, the user information is processed and aggregated to create 'algorithmic identities' that can be manipulated further for the purposes of third parties. Giving the sensitivity of the information that Ann handles, there are many ethical and other issues to be considered in connection to the use of cloud services.

A traditional shared information storage for many organizations has over the years been the company library or archive, which once consisted completely of physical materials that needed to be accessed in the location of the library or the archive. Gradually the libraries and archives are being digitised, alongside the development of digital record management systems, and today they often cover a combination of printed and digital content. They also do not consist of one single system, but of several, including new and updated systems as well as legacy systems, ones that are no longer maintained. The separate systems can create silos, where useful information for many purposes is locked behind limited access or from which it cannot be migrated. Consequently, different retrieval systems may be necessary to manage different parts of the collection. Some information systems, like company intranets, may contain heterogeneous types of material and unstructured content, such as organizational news, tests and experiments or guides on how to perform specific tasks, but also at least partially structured content on products, projects and persons, to which more or less advanced metadata is attached. To access this varied content has necessitated development of specific tools for searching information within the organization. The enterprise search engine mimics the search engines in the pubic internet in attempting to deal with a large variety of structured as well as unstructured material, but limiting the search to material that is only available internally (Kruschwitz and Hull, 2017, 1). The broad scope of unstructured materials included has been found to cause trouble for the functionality of these systems and management of the materials in general (cf. Chapter 4, 'Information management'). Among the tougher challenges for enterprise search systems is to develop algorithms that can take into consideration the variety of document formats and scale up to handle the document collection. Whereas metadata is often seen as a solution to enterprise search problems, few, if any, organizations are in a position to make full use of metadata, due to the high costs of creating and maintaining it. Schymik et al. (2015), on the other hand, argue that relatively simple metadata structures can facilitate enterprise search. Dumais et al. (2016) add that whereas most information retrieval technologies aim to discover information, much information searching focuses on finding and re-using previously seen information (cf. Jones, 2007). However, whilst finding or locating information itself is a challenge, it is accompanied by other related ones: for instance, from the perspective of archiving, questions of authenticity represent a challenge, and from the perspective of security, authorisation is an additional one (cf. Chapter 4, 'Information management'). Ann may have access, for example, only to the records of her own patients, which may not be available to her colleagues.

In sum, any workplace has several information artefacts, developed and used for different purposes. Any point of care or any other work duty that Ann gets involved with may result in an interaction with multiple information artefacts. For instance, the patient's body, her next-door colleague and the Medline database can all be useful information artefacts when she has to prescribe a medication. When she needs to fill out a travel reimbursement, she will turn to other types of information artefacts, such as the hospital's intranet, albeit possibly again also to her next-door colleague to ask for instructions. When participating in a research project, she consults the librarian at the hospital library on conducting a systematic search and deliberates with her international colleagues over the internet about their main findings. Indeed, the information artefacts and the needs for information in a workplace are varied. Cleverly and Burnett (2015) identified seven different facets when studying the information needs expressed by employees: broad, rich, intriguing, descriptive, general, expert and situational. Ann's work tasks are likely to prompt all of these types.

Information artefacts and information needs

In the above, we have discussed a number of different artefacts and their characteristics and use, we have illustrated how 'man-made' tools indeed are much more complex and diverse than they seem at first sight. A database, a tractor and an injection needle are more than just tools to store a piece of information, to plough up a field or to give a vaccination. They indicate a way of working, information and knowledge requirements for getting the work done, and sometimes they even indicate what work there is to be done. The relationship between (information) artefacts for work and the work itself is iterative, forming a two-way interdependency between them (cf. Orlikowski, 2010). For example, assuming that farmers will need to keep on cultivating their fields, but that tractor technology follows a similar development to lawn mowers, which the car industry is presently occupied with, the farmer will not need to sit on the tractor and drive it on the fields in the future. Instead, she will control the machine from a distance, only getting involved when the pre-programmed route scheme is invalid or the machine breaks down. This changes her work practices and her needs for information. Similar technological development has changed Ann's work practices, where both the knowledge of patients' bodies and the opportunities to respond to disorders of different kinds have increased tremendously. This means that Ann is as dependent on learning new ways to carry out her work as on her experience and tacit knowledge, perhaps even more so. Information artefacts have an immediate effect on her work, and in the trajectory of her work practices, they accentuate and lessen in significance, reflecting and emphasising the value of certain information and knowledge differently over time.

Information needs can be seen as a crucial link between information artefacts and work. It is often assumed that information needs are by definition something that are discovered, created and developed out of the immediate situation a person faces; as if Ann, while treating a patient who says her heart is beating fast, at that very moment discovers that she needs to measure the patient's electrical manifestations of heart activity. Instead, this request for information is a standard procedure for all physicians like Ann. Similarly, to expect that information artefacts are solely chosen for use based on their accessibility and suitability for the information need (i.e. Ann ordering an electrocardiogram for the patient) is somewhat oversimplified. This relation is more likely to be of the kind where the information artefacts through their availability lead to certain types of information needs, that is, to needs that are possible to satisfy by using the information artefacts available. Thus, it is not *only* the situation at hand, but also the information artefacts available, that influence how information needs are generated and perceived. Such an iterative, rather than linear, relationship is likely to be the case when considering any type of information need, but particularly so in work environments.

Both information needs and information artefacts are produced over time in the cultural-historical trajectory of work, where practices to perform work through a set of work tasks are legitimised as part of professional and/or organizational distinction. As a recent development in a long line of research on professions, Wenger-Trayner and Wenger-Trayner (2014) refer to a regime of competence, where members are accountable for their performance within their communities, such as professional groups or work organizations. Such performance includes the recognition of information requirements and needs and suitable information and its sources and channels. This means, furthermore, that the problems and their resolutions are formed in relation to information made available and deemed legitimate to use, unconsciously or consciously, within the bound-aries of what is considered to belong to the sphere of a given profession or organization (cf. Taylor, 1991). In the case of the example of the farmer and her tractor above, as well as to our cardiologist Ann, as sophisticated digital information artefacts increasingly support many professions, some work tasks will disappear and new ones replace them as a consequence of such automation of work-related information and other activities (cf. Chapter 2, 'Information work'). New information requirements and needs surface, partly out of the tasks but also out of the information (made) available.

In Figure 5.1 on the next page the downward arrow demonstrates the point of use of an information artefact as it is characterised by a number of features on the trajectory of time on collective and personal dimensions. In sum, we define information artefacts broadly as means to facilitate fulfilling informational requirements at work. In this chapter, we have discussed the key conceptualisations of information artefacts from the perspectives of workers and their workplaces: information sources,

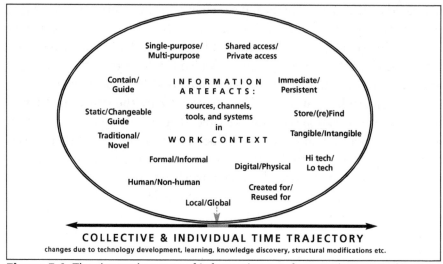

Figure 5.1 *The situated agency of information artefacts at the point of use*

information channels, information tools, information systems, social media and enterprise search systems. Both the worker and the workplace have a history of experiences, knowledge, rules and regulations, etc. in partly shared, partly separate contexts resulting in partly shared, partly separate understandings, motivations and goals. Information artefacts are constructed and reconstructed as they are used on these time trajectories. As such they are sensitive to changes occurring, for instance, on the basis of technological development, learning, innovations in the ways of adding value to information, new knowledge enactments and/or establishing or reorganizing relationships in the work setting. Each information artefact can be described by a number of features, or continuums, that modify – that is, have agency in – how information-related activities, such as information needs, searching and seeking, play out in performing work. Information artefacts may provide immediate or persistent content, depending on whether the very same content can be reused; they can be created for a specific purpose, but used for several others; they can have other origins than that of informational purposes; they can be digital or physical, static or constantly revised, formal or informal, etc. In Figure 5.1, we have captured the key information artefacts and a number of defining features discussed in the present chapter. Our selection of information artefacts is undoubtedly small, given the broadness of our definition, and there are many more interesting and important information artefacts to be identified and studied in any workplace. However, we have been able to demonstrate the diversity of the kinds of information artefacts in use in a workplace, including uncontested ones such as a medical record or a collaboration tool as well as more controversial ones such as a patient or a doctor.

Conclusions: information artefacts, collegial inclusion and expertise in the workplace

Research that focuses on the use of information sources and that takes information needs as an isolated phenomenon is often criticised, and quite rightly so, for being simplistic. However, studying the use of information artefacts is clearly meaningful if their contextual multilateral relations are acknowledged. Within a workplace, this means that individual and socio-cognitive as well as material and socio-cultural aspects require attention in order to grasp the complexity of information artefacts.

Research within the field of workplace information is likely to further our understanding of the complexity of information artefacts. By granting information artefacts an agency of their own, several directions open up for future research. Automation of work tasks affects the way the work by Ann and others will develop, as will the information artefacts developed for these new ways of working. Among specific issues to consider in this respect are how expertise in workplaces develops and what kinds of conceptualisations of expertise are gaining ground. Traditionally it has been the generation with longer hands-on tacit experience at the workplace that has been considered as experts from whom the new generation learns. This type of experience-based expertise is now being contested with knowledge-based expertise that relates to competences to handle new knowledge, i.e. capacity to adjust to knowledge development. The former is often oriented towards preserving procedures found functional over time, whereas the latter focuses on assessing and if necessary changing organizational procedures, based on contemporary knowledge. Automation opens up a third kind of conceptualisation, which is a consequence of advances in artificial intelligence: an algorithmic expertise that is based on synth-etisation of huge amounts of inputs to an abridged result. This type of expertise is a result of modern information artefacts and differs fundamentally from the first two, which are based on human activity and mediation. The algorithmic expertise builds on non-human information processing, where complicated and endless calculations provide information that a human mind is unable to reduce back to its original components. Thus, users of information provided by algorithmic expertise may have difficulties in examining the correctness or appropriateness of the abridged results, which make them difficult to evaluate and legitimise in professional and organizational regimes of competence. How the workplace is able to co-ordinate the different conceptualisations of expertise and information artefacts related to them will pose a challenge, but also opportunity to elevate the overall knowledge base of the workplace.

Another area of work life where development of information artefacts is bound to make a difference is through infrastructure development. Despite the ethical, information security and other issues, cloud technology makes it possible to fully digitise our work environments – not perhaps in the very near future, but in due time more and more work duties will be possible to perform from a distance. Already much oral, visual and documented information can be shared digitally, and the supporting technology is more solid and precise. The technology development is likely to remain a constant but perhaps a lesser concern for how our work develops. Instead, consequences for the physical workplace and our understanding of work may become a greater concern and require novel solutions, too. Many workplaces still rely heavily on the physical proximity of their workforce to co-ordinate and consolidate work activity and relationships between peers. Many work tasks can be carried out in a similar manner despite the physical distance; others need more adjustments, but are basically the same. However, since industrialisation some 200 years ago, the workplace has been defined as the physical place to carry out work in parallel or together with others, and the socio-cultural tradition to 'go to work' has grown strong. It will be a challenge to both employees and employers to find socially acceptable and rewarding alternative ways of working and building work communities. The ways in which information artefacts facilitate or hinder the bridging between physical and digital workplaces concerning collegial inclusion at work are likely to become one important future area of research on information artefacts within workplace information.

We have but touched upon the complexity of information artefacts in this chapter. We have argued for a more elaborated view of information artefacts than that of neutral means to get the work done. In our view they are an incremental part of the work itself, well worth studying in a diversity of workplaces.

References

Allen, T. J. (1969) *Roles in Technical Communication Networks*, working paper, Sloan School of Management, Cambridge, MA, MIT.

Baeza-Yates, R. and Ribeiro-Neto, B. (2011) *Modern Information Retrieval: the concepts and technology behind search*, ACM Press Books.

Billett, S. (2004) Workplace Participatory Practices: conceptualising workplaces as learning environments, *Journal of Workplace Learning*, **16** (6), 312–24.

Brown, J. S. and Duguid, P. (2017) *The Social Life of Information: updated, with a new preface*, Harvard Business Review Press.

Byström, K. and Hansen, P. (2005) Conceptual Framework for Tasks in Information Studies, *Journal of the Association for Information Science and Technology*, **56** (10), 1050–61.

Byström, K. and Järvelin, K. (1995) Task Complexity Affects Information Seeking and Use, *Information Processing and Management*, **31** (2), 191–213.

Berg, M. and Bowker, G. (1997) The Multiple Bodies of the Medical Record, *Sociological Quarterly*, **38** (3), 513–37.

Case, D. O. and Given, L. M. (2016) *Looking for Information: a survey of research on information seeking, needs, and behavior*, 4th edn, Elsevier/Academic Press.

Chang, Y. (2016) Influence of Human Behavior and the Principle of Least Effort on Library and Information Science Research, *Information Processing and Management*, **52** (4), 658–69.

Cleverley, P. H. and Burnett, S. (2015) Retrieving Haystacks: a data driven information needs model for faceted search, *Journal of Information Science*, **41** (1), 97–113.

Daft, R. L. and Lengel, R. H. (1986) Organizational Information Requirements, Media Richness and Structural Design, *Management Science*, **32** (5), 554–71.

Davies, E. and McKenzie, P. J. (2004) Preparing for the Opening Night: temporal boundary objects in textually-mediated professional practice, *Information Research*, **10** (1) paper 211, www.informationr.net/ir/10-1/paper211.html.

Dumais, S., Cutrell, E., Cadis, J. J., Jancke, G., Sarin, R. and Robbins, D. C. (2016) Stuff I've Seen: a system for personal information retrieval and re-use, *ACM SIGIR Forum*, **49** (2), 28–35.

Forsgren, E. and Byström, K. (2018) Multiple Social Media in the Workplace: contradictions and congruencies, *Information Systems Journal*, **28** (3), 442–64.

Giddens, A. (1984) *The Construction of Society*, University of California Press.

Gordon, M. D. (1997) It's 10 am. Do You Know Where Your Documents Are? The nature and scope of information retrieval problems in business, *Information Processing and Management*, **33** (1), 107–22.

Hardy, A. P. (1982) The Selection of Channels When Seeking Information: cost/benefit vs least-effort, *Information Processing and Management*, **18** (6), 289–93.

Hertzum, M. (2014) Expertise Seeking: a review, *Information Processing and Management*, **50** (5), 775–95.

Huvila, I. (2013) How a Museum Knows? Structures, work roles, and infrastructures of information work, *Journal of the American Society for Information Science and Technology*, **64** (7), 13.

Huvila, I., Enwald, H., Eriksson-Backa, K., Hirvonen, N., Nguyen, H. and Scandurra, I. (2018) Anticipating Ageing: older adults reading their medical records, *Information Processing and Management*, **54** (3), 394–407.

Jarrahi, M. H. and Thomson, L. (2017) The Interplay Between Information Practices and Information Context: the case of mobile knowledge workers, *Journal of the Association for Information Science and Technology*, **68** (5), 1073–89.

Jones, W. (2007) Personal Information Management, *Annual Review of Information Science and Technology*, **41** (1), 453–504.

Jung, Y. and Lyytinen, K. (2014) Towards an Ecological Account of Media Choice: a case study on pluralistic reasoning while choosing e-mail, *Information Systems Journal*, **24** (3), 271–93.

Kelly, D. (2009) Methods for Evaluating Interactive Information Retrieval Systems with Users, *Foundations and Trends in Information Retrieval*, **3** (1–2), 1–224.

Kruschwitz, U. and Hull, C. (2017) Searching the Enterprise, *Foundations and Trends in Information Retrieval*, **11** (1), 1–142.

Lancaster, F. W. (1991) *Indexing and Abstracting in Theory and Practice*, 3rd edn, Facet Publishing.

Leonardi, P. M. (2015) Ambient Awareness and Knowledge Acquisition: using social media to learn 'who knows what' and 'who knows whom', *MIS Quarterly*, **39** (4), 747–62.

Lindh, M. and Nolin, J. (2016) Information We Collect: surveillance and privacy in the implementation of Google Apps for Education, *European Educational Research Journal*, **15** (6), 644–63.

Lloyd, A. (2006) Information Literacy Landscapes: an emerging picture, *Journal of Documentation*, **62** (5), 570–83, doi.org/10.1108/00220410610688723.

McKenzie, P. J. (2015) Genre and Typified Activities in Informing and Personal Information Management. In Andersen, J. (ed.), *Genre Theory in Information Studies*, Emerald Publishing, 67–90.

Noël, S. and Robert, J. M. (2003) How the Web is Used to Support Collaborative Writing, *Behaviour and Information Technology*, **22** (4), 245–62.

Nordsteien, A. and Byström, K. (2018) Transitions in Workplace Information Practices and Culture: the influence of newcomers on information use in healthcare, *Journal of Documentation*, **74** (4), 827–43.

O'Reilly, C. A. (1982) Variations in Decision Makers' Use of Information Sources: the impact of quality and accessibility of information, *Academy of Management Journal*, **25** (4), 756–71.

Orlikowski, W. J. (2010) The Sociomateriality of Organizational Life: considering technology in management research, *Cambridge Journal of Economics*, **34** (1), 125–41.

Orlikowski, W. J. and Yates, J. (1994) Genre Repertoire: the structuring of communicative practices in organizations, *Administrative Science Quarterly*, **39**, 541–74.

Paisley, W. J. (1968) Information Needs and Uses, *Annual Review of Information Science and Technology*, **3** (1), 1–30.

Pharo, N. and Järvelin, K. (2006) 'Irrational' Searchers and IR-rational Researchers, *Journal of the American Society for Information Science and Technology*, **57** (2), 222–32.

Pilerot, O. (2014) Making Design Researchers' Information Sharing Visible Through Material Objects, *Journal of the Association for Information Science and Technology*, **65** (10), 2006–16.

Ruthven, I. (2008) Interactive Information Retrieval, *Annual Review of Information Science and Technology*, **42** (1), 43–91.

Salancik, G. R. and Pfeffer, J. (1978) A Social Information Processing Approach to Job Attitudes and Task Design, *Administrative Science Quarterly*, **23**, 224–53.

Schymik, G., Corral, K., Schuff, D. and Louis, R. (2015) The Benefits and Costs of Using Metadata to Improve Enterprise Document

Search, *Decision Sciences*, **46** (6), 1049–75.

Smith, C. L. and Kantor, P. B. (2008) User Adaptation: good results from poor systems. In *Proceedings of the 31st Annual International ACM SIGIR Conference on Research and Development in Information Retrieval*, ACM, 147–54.

Stenmark, D. (2010) Information Seeking in Organizations: a comparative survey of intranet usage. In *Proceedings of the 16th Americas Conference on Information Systems (AMCIS)*, Lima, Peru, August 12–15, 2010.

Taylor, R. S. (1991) Information Use Environments, *Progress in Communication Sciences*, **10**, 217–55.

Teevan, J., Alvarado, C., Ackerman, M. S. and Karger, D. R. (2004) The Perfect Search Engine is Not Enough: a study of orienteering behavior in directed search. In *Proceedings of the SIGCHI Conference on Human Factors in Computing Systems*, ACM, 415–22.

Treem, J. W. and Leonardi, P. M. (2013) Social Media Use in Organizations: exploring the affordances of visibility, editability, persistence, and association, *Annals of the International Communication Association*, **36** (1), 143–89.

Veinot, T. C. (2007) 'The Eyes of the Power Company': workplace information practices of a vault inspector, *Library Quarterly*, **77** (2), 157–79.

Wenger-Trayner, E. and Wenger-Trayner, B. (2014) Learning in Landscapes of Practice: a framework. In Wenger-Trayner, E., Fenton-O'Creevy, M., Hutchinson, S., Kubiak, C. and Wenger-Trayner, B. (eds), *Learning in Landscapes of Practice: boundaries, identity, and knowledgeability in practice-based learning*, Routledge.

Widén-Wulff, G. (2007) Motives for Sharing: social networks as information sources. In *Advances in Library Administration and Organization*, Emerald, 1–31.

Wilczynski, N. L. and Haynes, R. B. (2009) Consistency and Accuracy of Indexing Systematic Review Articles and Meta analyses in Medline, *Health Information and Libraries Journal*, **26** (3), 203–10.

Wilson, T. D. (1999) Models in Information Behaviour Research, *Journal of Documentation*, **55** (3), 249–70.

Zmud, R. W. (1983) The Effectiveness of External Information Channels in Facilitating Innovation Within Software Development Groups, *MIS Quarterly*, **7** (2), 43–58.

6

Information attributes

Diane Rasmussen Pennington and Ian Ruthven

Introduction

Information attributes are everyday concepts and part of our everyday language when discussing information. When dealing with patient information Ann, our cardiologist, will care about issues such as the *novelty* of any information representing change in her patient's condition, its *accuracy* and the *quality* of the information she is receiving. Novelty can be assessed by the time of the information, recorded in a standard format that all medical staff use and understand, accuracy may be judged by knowledge of how the information was created and quality of information may be judged by who provided the information or how useful the information is in deciding how to treat her patients. Ann will also have to deal with various *genres* of information, such as patient records, heart rhythm traces, temperature charts, etc., which can be used for different purposes and to make different decisions. Many information attributes require high levels of domain knowledge to be used correctly; part of Ann's professional training dealt with how to read these documents and how to use them to treat her patients.

Our lawyer Johan will also interact with many types of information and care about issues of *bias* in the information, the degree to which his information can be *verified* with respect to other sources of information and whether he has *confidence* in his information source. In presenting evidence to the court he will need to consider whether his evidence is *clear*, if it provides *tangible* facts and whether it is *consistent* with other information being presented. Johan also needs to care about whether his own legal knowledge is *up to date*, whether his interpretation of the law is *consistent* with other lawyers and whether he is translating specialised information in such a way that his clients and the jury will have the *ability to understand* the information he is providing.

Liila, our journalist, has to deal with many sources of information, and she will also care about novelty of information and its accuracy but she also has concerns over whether the information is *recent*, whether her sources are *authoritative*, whether the information is sufficiently *specific* to her story and the *affective* nature of the information on her potential readers. She may also have to care about the *cost* of information, whether information is *available* in time for her deadline, whether the information she is getting is *dynamic* and therefore does she have to keep updating her story and maybe issues such as whether the information only covers a certain *geographic area*. She will also care about whether the information she needs is *findable* with the tools she uses in her daily work.

Ann, Johan and Liila all care about the same thing – is their information *good* information? Their differing work roles mean that what they see as 'good' information will change depending on their uses of information. The italicised words in the preceding examples are indications of kinds of information attributes we can use when assessing the information we have available. In the rest of this chapter, we expand on this core idea that we can assess information by attributes of the information and information objects to understand how others might make these decisions, and to improve the design of information systems that provide better support for making these decisions. We use the term 'objects' to refer to the narrow concept of storable and findable items, a subset of the wider concept of information artefacts from the previous chapter.

Theoretical underpinnings

Maron noted in an early information science contribution that 'Information is not a stuff' (Maron, 1965). However, it is often treated as such, with many papers written in information seeking, information management and information use that treat information as a vague generic thing that we create, search for, use or disseminate, without ever specifying what type of information is being created, searched, disseminated or used or what form that information takes. This is unsatisfying on many levels; not least because it creates an imprecision in our understanding of what is happening with information in workplace settings and what types of information are being used for what purposes.

This has led to many serious, but perhaps inconclusive, attempts to define what is meant by this thing we call 'information' (e.g. Weaver, 1949; Fritz Machlup, 1983; Shannon, 2001; Cornelius, 2002; Capurro and Hjørland, 2003). These definitional approaches frequently remain abstract and lack operational power to move us forward in understanding what it is we do with information in real environments. No single definition has really stuck and the debate rolls on over what we mean by information. Possibly, because 'information' itself is so complex and difficult to define, it is also challenging to identify a set list of attributes or characteristics that can be used to describe information. The following sections cover tangible as well as more abstract notions of the qualities used in information science research to describe the attributes collectively comprising the concept of information: objects, properties and relevance.

Objects

Even if we can't agree on the meaning of 'information', what information science has successfully done is provide ways to classify information sources and *objects* to create a vocabulary around objects, their organization and use. We can perform this classification in two ways: by characterising properties of the information objects such as documents, video and e-mail, or by properties of the information we obtain from these objects.

Information objects have many useful properties that can help us access, use and discuss information. Factual, if sometimes controversial, properties, such as source, age, language and type, can provide useful metadata for querying. The objects' contents can provide the raw material for indexing schemes to allow end-user searching. Usage statistics can provide the basis for recommender systems and for quality metrics such as impact factors. The different natures of objects can lead to systematised forms to which we ascribe names such as 'memo', 'report', 'brochures', 'press releases', etc., and which help us understand what objects we are interacting with.

We can also create algorithms to help us assign attributes to information objects, for example based on the level of textual complexity or readability level, and there is a rich stream of such research seeking to analyse information automatically to provide new features for searching and browsing.

Properties and relevance

A separate stream of research is in describing information by what we see as *properties* of the information we obtain from interacting with these objects, e.g. the value of the information to us – a subjective concept compared to the more objective concept of cost. Many of these properties are relations between us and the information objects we are dealing with. This idea of looking at what characteristics we use to decide whether information is relevant to our needs was investigated robustly by Barry and Schamber in two studies, both based on workplace information seeking (Barry, 1994; Barry and Schamber, 1998; Schamber, 1991). Their investigations showed that there is a large set of relevance criteria, or values that people use to decide on relevance, and that these criteria are a mixture of object properties (such as source), information properties (such as validity of the information) and personal properties (such as ability of the user to understand the information). Further studies have demonstrated that different relevance criteria may be used in different workplace settings but that they form a stable core of decisions we make about information and information objects.

The concept of relevance itself is an important one, as workplace tasks are built around being able to access relevant, rather than just any, information. Relevance is another term that has at the same time too many and too few definitions; too many that we can confidently say what it means and too few that operationalise it in a way that we can confidently measure. Nevertheless, there are some useful definitions. In 1975, Saracevic claimed that information science 'emerged as the third subject, along with logic and philosophy, to deal with relevance . . . Relevance is considered as a measure of the effectiveness of a context between a source and a destination in a communication process' (Saracevic, 1975). Later, in 1996, Saracevic presented five contrasting definitions of relevance (Saracevic, 1996).

1 *System relevance*, or the relationship between the representation of an information object and the representation of a user's search request within a given information system. In some ways this is the lowest meaning of relevance, as it is based on algorithmic matching or similarity, but it is a very common way of interacting with information. This level says nothing about an object beyond its content.

2 *Topical or subject relevance*, which is the relationship between the topic of the information object and the topic of the user's search request. This goes beyond information that is contained within the object to what the object is 'about' at a more thematic level. This 'aboutness' may be inferred from external sources such as user-generated content but still stays at the content level. In both system and topical relevance, the indexable properties of the objects are important.

3 *Cognitive relevance*, or the relationship between the state of knowledge and needs of the user and the texts (rather than the representation of the texts). Here what is important is not just content but also issues such as novelty, quality and the ability to understand the material with which we are interacting.

4 *Situational relevance*, or the relationship between the situation and the information objects are key here. What is relevant is what helps us in progressing through a situation and this may be about better decision making, problem solving or establishing precedent. Situational factors can therefore include issues about cost of information or findability of information that vary across situations.

5 *Motivational relevance*, or the relationship between the goals of the user and the information objects. This goes beyond moving ahead in a situation to thinking about issues such as satisfaction with how a situation has been tackled. At this highest level of relevance, we see issues that relate to preferences and motivations that will relate to aspects such as the complexity of information, or its readability or affective issues, such as how interesting texts are to read.

Therefore, different levels relate to different attributes of information objects: lower levels such as the system level involve simple, although easily manipulated, properties of objects such as content, whereas higher levels involve attributes that require more complex system support. This support may come in the form of more sophisticated indexing features, such as the algorithms used in music retrieval to classify music by mood or genre, or in the form of improved interactive support. This support can involve making available more information to the user, which, in turn, gives more power to make better decisions. We already see different information attributes being surfaced in different applications: price, origin, seller feedback for online shopping sites, for example, or in the case of video sites, making available information on the number of views, source, popularity, etc., which can be used to help assign values to the various relevance criteria which a user may be working with.

Relevance is not the only factor influencing users' selection of sources. For example, an additional one is the objective *cost* of information. Hardy analysed the cost/benefit model of selecting information sources, which 'proposes that information seekers select information sources on the basis of expected benefits and expected costs of using an information source' (Hardy, 1982, 289). In his study of forestry workers, costs were much more important than benefits in source selection.

There are many information attributes. In what follows we present an analysis of some of them to illustrate the range of research in this area. We look at classical attributes, such as complexity; attributes, such as genre, that are being constantly redefined; and new attributes, such as findability, that are arising from the need to have new ways of thinking about information in new information environments.

Genre

A document's genre, or what type of document it is, can influence whether a workplace user believes a retrieved document is relevant and where to look for information in the first place. For example, if software developers want to know how other developers wrote code for a particular situation, discussion forums will be more helpful than vendors' manuals. In other words, the task the worker needs to complete influences what type of document is needed (Freund et al., 2005).

Genre can be described as a set of texts that share a purpose as identified by the community which produces or uses them (Swales, 1990). Yates and Orlikowski (1992) stated that 'genres are social institutions that are produced, reproduced, or modified when human agents draw on genre rules to engage in organizational communication'. That is, groups of people working together create document *types* to help them communicate for different purposes and these types tell us something about what each group of people see as important to completing their tasks or, as Watt (2009) has observed, 'convergence on a set of standardised document structures is both natural and helpful'. We can see genres developing over time in information repositories as authors gradually develop information structures to help readers find information easily within articles (Clark et al., 2009).

There is also evidence from eye-tracking studies that genre familiarity reduces the cognitive effort in analysing texts (Clark et al., 2014).

Freund et al. (2006) studied software engineers to develop a taxonomy of 16 genres for documents, including manuals, presentations, product documents, tech notes/tips, tutorials and labs, white papers, best practices, design patterns, discussions/forums, cookbooks and guides, engagement summaries, problem reports and technical articles. Other disciplines have their own standard and emerging genres that are important to understand and be able to use in order to become part of that discipline or profession.

Some work-related genres seem universal: lectures, user manuals, company reports, journal articles, etc., will be instantly recognisable across cultures and organizations. Others may be entering history as they disappear from use. The memorandum pinned to the company noticeboard was at one time a critical means of disseminating instruction and information. Now, e-mail and texting have almost eliminated this type of communication. Equally, new developments create new genres such as webinars, vlogs and tweets that have to be blended into institutions' information activities and require learning by individual workers and entire institutions on how to best use them.

In many areas of work life, there are particular types of genre that only those in that area truly understand how to create and read. The 'convergence' of a community into Watt's 'standardised document structure' makes it easier for those working in a work community to communicate better and work more efficiently but makes it harder for those outside to understand and access information. Certain areas of work, such as the legal field, with its case notes, affidavits, summons, subpoenas, plaint notes, contracts, etc., are so rich in genre that we often need professional intermediaries, such as journalists, to explain what it all means.

Genres can provide the basis for information organization in many workplaces. Sometimes it is as simple as having all staff records in one filing cabinet and all invoices in another one. For larger institutions there will be often more sophisticated support, including specialist IT systems, for storing and searching within and across genres, and we may have specialist sub-units like human resources teams who take charge of developing particular genres and their deployment within institutions.

Genres make it easier for us to know where to start looking for information: if Ann, our cardiologist, wants to learn about new treatments for heart disease she knows to start with recent medical journals rather than post-mortem reports. The 'standardised document structures' highlighted by Watt make it easier to create IT systems to support our access to information by allowing us to search with this structure or to use the structure to perform textual analyses like summarisation.

Complexity

Some information we find easy to follow; some we struggle to understand. If we cannot understand information, or rather cannot understand it quickly or easily enough for our purposes, then we may reject it altogether. For the purposes of this chapter, we will refer to the *complexity* of information as denoting how easy or difficult it is to follow. This doesn't help explain what complexity is and, as in most fields, it can mean different things but it does denote the general sense of 'hardness', 'challenge' or 'difficulty' of some texts over others.

Complexity is usually a relation between the person reading a document and the document they are reading. We may find one document to be complex but you do not, as you have more experience in that area, or more familiarity with the vocabulary used in the text than we have. Experience and practice does count and Liila's long experience of reading court reports will give her an advantage over a more junior reporter in knowing which parts of the document to read first, what to look for in the document and what various concepts mean. Complexity, therefore, is relative to the person doing the reading.

However, complexity has an objective side as well. There are many tests of so-called 'readability' that attempt to measure how difficult texts may be to read based on textual features such as sentence length, word length and word frequencies. One of the more famous ones, the Flesch reading-ease test, gives higher scores to material that is seen as being easier to read. A score of 90–100 denotes text that is very easy to read and seen as easily understood by an average 11-year-old, whereas a score of 0–30 indicates text that is difficult to read and most suitable for those with university-level education. This chapter has a Flesch reading-ease score of 32.9, so well done if you are still managing to follow us.

A related test, the Flesch-Kincaid Grade Level test, maps scores from similar textual features onto education levels, indicating what level of education is necessary to read the text. Although criticised by some for being overly simplistic, these readability scores have been influential in encouraging analyses of whether information provided by certain organizations is too complex. In some cases, this has led to laws to ensure that information by some companies, e.g. by insurance companies, is at the right level of complexity to be understood by most of their customers.

Low complexity is not a desired result in all cases. Van Der Sluis et al., for example, have shown that newspaper articles that are too simple are just as likely to be rated as uninteresting as articles that are too difficult to read, suggesting complexity is balanced against other factors when deciding what information we prefer (Van der Sluis et al., 2014). There is indeed a tension around communication in workplace environments regarding the complexity of information; we know experts can deal with complex information more effectively than novices and information that is insufficiently succinct is annoying. However, if information is too complex then we reduce the number of people who can deal with it.

Novelty

Barry and Schamber (1998) distinguished between three different types of novelty: content, source and document novelty. Content novelty is the extent to which the information presented is novel to the user, source novelty the extent to which a source of the document (i.e. author, journal) is novel to the user and document novelty the extent to which the document itself is novel to the user. These are all related to the user of the information and their current state of knowledge; we may also add in recency or the extent to which information is recent, current or up to date – a more objective notion of novel.

The ability to distinguish what is new is critical to many workplace environments: Ann needs to keep up to date with the latest medical knowledge, Johan needs to know what laws are current to be able to adequately defend his clients and Liila's whole occupation is based around what is 'new(s)'. For many workplaces, keeping up to date with the latest information and having a good range of high-quality information sources is essential to competitive success and attention has to be given to how to ensure workers are kept up to date. For all organizations there is also a requirement to keep up to date with compliance issue such as health and safety, tax laws and other business purposes.

How we keep up to date shows a variety of practices. In academic work, journals and conferences are standard ways to recognise the latest findings in a research field. But we have to know which conferences and journals to read or we may miss important information. We also need to know how to select which are the best ones to read. Those who are better connected will also know which sources of research information are doing the best research and may have indirect connections to these researchers to get highlights before they become official literature. In other areas, such as journalism, having good sources of information that can guarantee the latest information is also a critical advantage.

In other fields, particularly entrepreneurial areas, *being* novel is crucial. Investing in a new product could be a complete waste of time and resources if a rival has already patented the idea. In areas such as intellectual property search (or patent searching), search success is the confidence that one has not found a previous patent (Trippe and Ruthven, 2011), i.e. success can be defined as the failure to find relevant information. However, knowing that we have failed to find information because it does not exist – no one else has patented our idea – rather than because we have just searched ineffectively can never be properly resolved. Several studies, including influentially Blair and Maron (1985), have indicated that we are not very good at telling whether we have all the information that we need when searching.

Metrics

With so much information available, we need ways to help decide where to focus our attention. One approach is to employ metrics or quantitative measures as surrogates for quality or popularity and for other purposes. A variety of metrics exist to track and describe information. Metrics allow owners and users of information to answer a variety of questions about how the information is used and who is using it. There are many terms for this area: 'bibliometrics', 'scientometrics', 'informetrics', 'webometrics', etc., but what they all share is a concern over what data we use to create metrics, what they represent and their reliability for decision making.

For academics, bibliometrics is a field of research within information science that 'boils down to the quantitative analysis of published scholarly literature, notably journal articles and the network of their bibliographic connections' (De Bellis, 2014, 23). Bibliometric information allows researchers to track the reach of their research, such as how many times their papers have been cited, the disciplines of the authors that have cited them and so on.

Traditional metrics, such as impact factors, are being challenged by new types of media with their own metrics, such as a scholar's number of Twitter followers, number of likes on a Facebook post linking to a newly published journal article, etc. (Cronin and Sugimoto, 2014). Altmetrics is an approach to tracking newer and previously unnoticed or non-existent forms of research impact, such as how many times an article is mentioned on Twitter, or how many blog posts discuss it (Priem, 2014).

Both within and outside academia, social media encompass a massive amount of metrics. Some are available to the user, and some are not. For example, on Facebook, users can see how many times their posts are liked, shared, commented on and viewed. Facebook's algorithms track what posts users view and whom they interact with most often; users do not see these metrics themselves, but the metrics do influence what users see in their Facebook feed.

Organizations can gather and analyse website metrics through simple programs that exist on their servers, or with external services such as Google Analytics. These programmes provide a plethora of details, such as how their users found their pages, the process each user followed while progressing through the site, how long they spent on each page and much more. These metrics are useful to understand what parts of a website its visitors value as well as where they might get frustrated and therefore leave the site.

How might metrics influence the use of workplace information? Consider a corporate intranet containing, in part, a library of documents that staff need to do their work. If staff can see how often everyone has accessed each document, a high accession rate might influence their decision to choose a particular document, because the ones used the most are likely to be the most useful and current.

Authority

The authority of an author or other information creator is an important attribute of information. It is essential for a critical reader to consider if and why a given creator is the right person to provide given information. In a time when 'alternative facts' and 'fake news' have become common terms, it is difficult to know whom to trust. The authority of a creator is probably related to the reliability and quality of information provided. These are important attributes for people as they decide whether to use information based on its trustworthiness and/or whether it is relevant to their needs. In a seminal study (Rieh, 2002, 145), users' judgements of online quality and authority 'were identified in terms of characteristics of information objects, characteristics of sources, knowledge, situation, ranking in search output, and general assumption'.

Cognitive authority is one measure of authority, which is defined as the extent to which people think they can trust information based on who wrote it or where it is published (Wilson, 1983). For example, if physicians are seeking updated information about a condition, they will probably think new research published in a top medical journal is a more authoritative choice for making decisions about treatments for the condition than patients' blogs about their personal experiences with the disease. Before the internet, it was perhaps easier to determine cognitive authority, because apparently reliable sources were in printed form, such as a book, a journal, an encyclopaedia, or any other resource found in a library. The librarians chose the most reliable sources based on the author's reputation, the credibility of the publisher, and so on. It is no longer possible to make these relatively straightforward decisions.

In today's online environment where anyone can create and post information, it has become more difficult to ascertain cognitive authority, and new models of authority need to be negotiated (Neal, 2010). Neal and McKenzie performed discourse analysis on blog posts written by women with the female chronic illness known as endometriosis, to examine how women make decisions about the authority of information about the disease and its possible treatments. From the research, they found a different type of authority, which they coined 'affective authority', as 'the extent to which users think the information is subjectively appropriate, empathetic, emotionally supportive, and/or aesthetically pleasing' (Neal and McKenzie, 2011, 131). Examples included information about the lived experience of particular treatments from other women with endometriosis as shared on blogs and discussion forums, the sensitive approach of a religious leader, or an understanding friend. While these figures do not have authority in Wilson's cognitive sense, they did provide substantial affective authority to the women in the study.

In a case study of environmental activists, participants' personal perceptions of media credibility and cognitive authority were essential to judging and selecting information sources; environmental agencies were seen as most credible, while newspapers were seen as less credible due to bias

(Savolainen, 2007). Wathen and Burkell (2001) performed a literature review regarding what factors influence judgements of the credibility of an online source. The answers were not straightforward; the factors included an entanglement of the source, the message, the institutional quality such as the owner of the website, and the receiver's perspective, such as information need, existing knowledge and social situation.

In any workplace setting, the authority of information consulted to perform a work task should be considered carefully. For example, for people in a new employment setting, it might be preferable to ask a superior for information until they know which peers are appropriately knowledgeable and approachable. Information stored on shared network drives or corporate intranets, although 'official' and institutionally supported, may be outdated, provide conflicting details or be presented to staff in a disorganized manner. It is then left to the member of staff to determine what version of a document is the most authoritative version (based on its currency, for example) before proceeding to use the information.

Findability

Another essential attribute of information is findability. If people cannot find information, they cannot use it, rendering it essentially worthless. Morville (2005, 4) provided three definitions of findability:

1 the quality of being locatable or navigable
2 the degree to which a particular object is easy to discover or locate
3 the degree to which a system or environment supports navigation and retrieval.

Imagine our lawyer Johan preparing for a trial. He needs to look up legal precedent that relates to the case. He knows the precedent exists, and it is probably in his firm's small legal library, but he does not remember the exact date of the ruling, and he cannot determine where to browse within the many volumes that could have the ruling in them. The information he needs is (probably) there, but it is not findable. He proceeds his preparation without the details he wanted.

Increasingly, however, the necessary information is stored online. People must rely on search engines such as Google to find what they need. Over time, the ability to find 'known items', such as when we know the title or part of the text, has improved substantially. For example, if Johan's precedent were available online, he could probably type the name of the case he wanted into a search engine and find it almost instantly.

Let us imagine that Johan knew he needed a previous case to discuss in court, and it existed online, but he did not know anything about it, such as its name or any text in it. What does he search for in order to find it? A classic problem inherent in search engines is that people must tell the search system what it is they do not know (Norman, 1988). In other words, it is difficult to find something when you do not know what it is.

The quality and amount of the organization and description of information within a search system greatly influences findability. For example, the way a website presents the structure of its information can influence whether someone finds needed information. If Ann, the cardiologist, needed to consult an online resource to ensure her prescribed dosage of a medication is correct for a patient, how should the site be organized? She might want to access the medication information by medication name, medication type, diagnosis, symptoms, potential side effects or a range of other facets that could sort and describe the medications. But if she goes to the resource, and the only way she can access information is through a very long page of medications, perhaps only sorted alphabetically, the resource is not organized well.

Closely related to the organization of information is its description. In traditional information science terms, bibliographic description of an item refers to a set of descriptors about the item, such as its title, author, date of publication, number of pages and so on; think about what descriptions library catalogues provide. Again, this is only helpful if you know some of the descriptive information for searching online resources. Many search engines solely or primarily search the descriptors in determining whether an item in the system matches the user's search. Additionally, the description tends to drive the organization of the system and its findability. Consider a department store's online shop. A person wants to find a women's red T-shirt in size 10 for under £20. The descriptions provided for all the shirts, as well as how the shirts matching her search return to her, determine findability. If the shirt she wants exists on the site, but she cannot find it, the shop will needlessly lose her business.

Information attributes can be used to create better interactive displays of information objects. Once we have attributes defined, we can create attractive and useful browsing systems to allow the user to narrow down the information they require by size, shape, colour, type, cost, origin, popularity or whatever attributes are meaningful and obtainable to that domain and set of information tasks. These displays and features improve findability because they allow users to determine what features are relevant to their needs.

Conclusion

Because information is hard to define, the characteristics of information also present a challenge to information science researchers and practitioners. Perhaps as the field continues to increase its understanding of what attributes are important to information users, it will be easier to define the vital attributes that emerge from information itself. Even if we agree on which attributes are important it can be a challenge to agree on how to measure an attribute such as complexity or authority.

It is worth noting that interactions performed on a document by its users can alter its attributes. In the internet age, people are able to add, edit and delete information attributes in previously impossible ways that can ultimately determine whether documents are retrieved. For example, the number of likes or favourites on a document posted on a social media website can influence its relevance ranking in the website's retrieval system (Neal, 2010). This is an important factor to consider in workplace settings as people increasingly use freely available social media resources such as YouTube in order to learn how to complete tasks or acquire new skills. Additionally, since so much information shared online is now in non-textual forms, such as videos, photographs, maps, music and so on, traditional attributes may need to be reconsidered and reconceptualised (Neal, 2012). It is perhaps not possible to represent important attributes of a visual document fully in words, since important features are lost in translation between word and image (O'Connor and Wyatt, 2004).

As we develop more ways to automatically process information, we see more and more indexing features being developed and included in algorithmic approaches to information retrieval and management. These do tend to be relatively low-level features. Higher-level ones, the ones used in Saracevic's higher relevance levels, remain difficult to operationalise, especially those that reflect more subjective assessments of information. Whilst we wait for algorithmic solutions to all information attributes there is a rich seam of useful research in developing interactive systems that support people making useful decisions on information attributes.

Some attributes require domain knowledge to be used effectively. Ann, Johan and Liila all care about issues such as authority, quality and accuracy of the information they use and will use their knowledge about sources, professional norms and how to interpret information to make such decisions. When we lack this domain knowledge, the evidence suggests we use different information attributes – ones we can more easily work with – to substitute for these 'expert' attributes. So, for example, if we cannot judge the accuracy of information in a document then we may look for evidence that other documents also contain the same information, i.e. the property that information can be verified, or we may look for the property of tangibility (containing concrete facts) to estimate accuracy (Wen and Ruthven, 2006). That is, we can be flexible about our decision making and which attributes to use based on the information we have available.

Information attributes are a fascinating area that informs us both about how people think and act on information as well as how we create information organization principles to support successful information interactions. As technology develops we see new forms of information develop, requiring new techniques for curating, assessing and working with these information objects, resulting in a very lively research area.

References

Barry, C. L. (1994) User-defined Relevance Criteria: an exploratory study, *Journal of the American Society for Information Science*, **45** (3), 149–59.

Barry, C. L. and Schamber, L. (1998) Users' Criteria for Relevance Evaluation: a cross-situational comparison, *Information Processing and Management*, **34** (2–3), 219–36.

Blair, D. C. and Maron, M. E. (1985) An Evaluation of Retrieval Effectiveness for a Full-text Document-retrieval System, *Communications of the ACM*, **28** (3), 289–99.

Capurro, R. and Hjørland, B. (2003) The Concept of Information, *Annual Review of Information Science and Technology*, **37** (1), 343–411.

Clark, M. J., Ruthven, I. and Holt, P. (2009) The Evolution of Genre in Wikipedia, *Journal for Language Technology and Computational Linguistics*, **25** (1), 1–22.

Clark, M., Ruthven, I., O'Brian Holt, P., Song, D. and Watt, S. (2014) You Have E-mail, What Happens Next? Tracking the eyes for genre, *Information*

Processing and Management, **50** (1) 175–98.

Cornelius, I. (2002) Theorising Information for Information Science, *Annual Review of Information Science and Technology,* **36** (1), 392–425.

Cronin, B. and Sugimoto, C. R. (2014) *Beyond Bibliometrics: harnessing multidimensional indicators of scholarly impact,* MIT Press.

De Bellis, N. (2014) History and Evolution of (Biblio)metrics. In Cronin, B. and Sugimoto, C. (eds), *Beyond Bibliometrics: harnessing multidimensional indicators of scholarly impact,* MIT Press, 23–44.

Freund, L., Toms, E. G. and Waterhouse, J. (2005) Modeling the Information Behaviour of Software Engineers Using a Work Task Framework, *Proceedings of the American Society for Information Science and Technology,* **42** (1), doi:10.1002/meet.14504201181.

Freund, L., Toms, E. G. and Waterhouse, J. (2006) Towards Genre Classification for IR in the Workplace. In *Proceedings of the 1st International Conference on Information Interaction in Context,* ACM, 30–36.

Fritz Machlup, U. M. (ed.) (1983) *Study of Information: interdisciplinary messages,* John Wiley & Sons.

Hardy, A. P. (1982) The Selection of Channels when Seeking Information: cost/benefit vs least-effort, *Information Processing and Management,* **18** (6), 289–93.

Maron, M. (1965) Mechanised Documentation: the logic behind a probabilistic. In *Statistical Association Methods for Mechanized Documentation: Symposium Proceedings,* US Government Printing Office.

Morville, P. (2005) *Ambient Findability: what we find changes who we become,* O'Reilly Media.

Neal, D. M. (2010) Emotion-based Tags in Photographic Documents: the interplay of text, image, and social influence/Les Étiquettes Basées sur des Émotions dans les Documents Photographiques: l'interaction entre le texte, l'image et l'influence sociale, *Canadian Journal of Information and Library Science,* **34** (3), 329–53.

Neal, D. and McKenzie, P. (2011) Putting the Pieces Together: endometriosis blogs, cognitive authority, and collaborative information behavior, *Journal of the Medical Library Association,* **99** (2), 127–34.

Neal, D. R. (2012) *Indexing and Retrieval of Non-text Information,* Walter de Gruyter.

Norman, D. (1988) *The Design of Everyday Things,* MIT Press.

O'Connor, B. C. and Wyatt, R. B. (2004) *Photo Provocations: thinking in, with, and about photographs*, Scarecrow Press.

Priem, J. (2014) Altmetrics. In *Beyond bibliometrics: harnessing multidimensional indicators of scholarly impact*, MIT Press, 263–88.

Rieh, S. Y. (2002) Judgment of Information Quality and Cognitive Authority in the Web, *Journal of the American Society for Information Science and Technology*, **53** (2), 145–61.

Saracevic, T. (1975) Relevance: a review of and a framework for the thinking on the notion in information science, *Journal of the American Society for Information Science*, **26** (6), 321–43.

Saracevic, T. (1996) Relevance Reconsidered. In *Proceedings of the Second Conference on Conceptions of Library and Information Science* (CoLIS 2), 201–18.

Savolainen, R. (2007) Media Credibility and Cognitive Authority: the case of seeking orienting information, *Information Research*, **12** (3), www.informationr.net/ir/12-3/paper319.html.

Schamber, L. (1991) Users' Criteria for Evaluation in a Multimedia Environment, *Proceedings of the 54th Annual Meeting of the American Society for Information Science*, 28, Learned Information, 126–33.

Shannon, C. E. (2001) A Mathematical Theory of Communication, *ACM SIGMOBILE Mobile Computing and Communications Review*, **5** (1), 3–55.

Swales, J. (1990) *Genre Analysis: English in academic and research settings*, Cambridge University Press.

Trippe, A. and Ruthven, I. (2011) Evaluating Real Patent Retrieval Effectiveness. In *Current Challenges in Patent Information Retrieval*, Springer, 125–43.

Van Der Sluis, F., van den Broek, E. L., Glassey, R. J., van Dijk, E. M. A. G. and de Jong, F. M. G. (2014) When Complexity Becomes Interesting, *Journal of the Association for Information Science and Technology*, **65** (7), 1478–500.

Wathen, C. N. and Burkell, J. (2001) Believe It or Not: factors influencing credibility on the web, *Journal of the American Society for Information Science and Technology*, **53** (2), 134–44.

Watt, S. (2009) *Text Categorisation and Genre in Information Retrieval*, John Wiley and Sons.

Weaver, W. (1949) The Mathematics of Communication, *Scientific American*, **181** (1), 11–15.

Wen, L., Ruthven, I. and Borlund, P. (2006) The Effects on Topic Familiarity on Online Search Behaviour and Use of Relevance Criteria. In Lalmas, M.,

MacFarlane, A., Rüger, S., Tombros, A., Tsikrika, T. and Yavlinsky, A. (eds), *Advances in Information Retrieval*, ECIR 2006, Lecture Notes in Computer Science, Vol. 3936. Springer.

Wilson, P. (1983) *Second-hand Knowledge: an inquiry into cognitive authority*, Greenwood Press.

Yates, J. and Orlikowski, W. J. (1992) Genres of Organizational Communication: a structurational approach to studying communication and media, *Academy of Management Review*, **17** (2), 299–326.

7

Workplace information environment – challenges and opportunities for research

Katriina Byström, Jannica Heinström, Ian Ruthven

Introduction

Work is central to most of what we care about as individuals and as communities. Work provides a sense of identity expressed through work roles; most of us would answer the question 'What are you?' with a line such as a 'I am a journalist/doctor/lawyer/regional manager/coastal zone advisor'. It provides a sense of purpose – 'I make sure the public is informed; I save lives; I help create a fair justice system; I make sure the environment is protected; I monitor our coastlines' – that may take years of training to achieve and must be constantly nurtured with new information. Work also provides economic gain that funds education, health services, the arts and most areas of civic life.

Work is central to how we organize many areas of our life. University and college training organizes us within disciplines and provides discipline-specific skills. Professional societies, guilds, trades, crafts and unions help us differentiate what is important and different about our work from that of other people. Even specialist buildings such as hospitals or schools encourage us to see some types of work as belonging in different spaces to other types of work. To do our work we need information. The work we do creates a specific filter for recognising important information for that work even during our leisure time and it creates information-related habits and awareness. A part of a journalist's identity, for example, is scanning for news, which may happen almost automatically and unintentionally during leisure. A doctor reads medical information with a different pre-understanding from that of a layperson. A lawyer picks up on trial-related news, while the regional manager learns to read natural signs that are invisible for someone without that filter. A part of the identity of a coastal zone advisor is an understanding of the natural environment. These information processes are often unconscious and not recognised. For work itself, however, these processes need to be made implicit and managed. Information science works to reveal, understand and implement more efficient information processes.

Information science studies work in many different ways; sometimes the focus is on higher-level socio-cultural aspects of workplace environments, sometimes the focus is on specific activities of curating or managing information and the systems that we use to perform these activities. In doing so, workplace information research takes influence from many allied disciplines, including management science, organizational studies, computer science, media studies, psychology and sociology.

Our aim in this book is to present the full spectrum of workplace information research, flowing from contributions on the nature of work when viewed from an information science perspective, through considerations of the social and cultural environments in which we work, to issues of managing our work and the information we need to do work, to discussions of the information artefacts and properties of those artefacts that enable us to 'work' with information to complete our 'work'. Implicit in all chapters is the worker him/herself, the person who does the work and interacts with all these levels in doing so. The social, cultural and material environment is a context of which the worker is part, and that is shaping and shaped by all individual players within it. Information management focuses on effective managerial processes so that each employee is able to use information most effectively for his/her work tasks. Artefacts and their properties, in turn, always play out in interaction with the worker and are used by him/her for diverse purposes of work.

One of the motivations for this book is that such topics are often considered separately, by distinct groupings of scholars, and appear in venues that offer little interaction between these topics. This, in part, comes from the perspective taken by individual authors – our disciplinary backgrounds bring their own theories, models and ways of looking at the world and, hence, different ways of approaching the study of information in the workplace. These different approaches can focus on different objects of study (environments, systems, tasks, objects, practices, etc.), some of which are more amenable to certain theories and ways of doing research than others. Each perspective is valuable in highlighting different aspects of what it means to study workplace information. Bringing these perspectives together in one text we hope will show the diversity in this rich area of study and promote new discussions on how we can appreciate these perspectives to create new ways of investigating and understanding different phenomena within the field of workplace information.

In this chapter, we return to Taylor's information use environments and, inspired by the chapters in this book, propose an extended model, the Workplace Information Environment model. In the concluding section, we outline some future direction for workplace information research.

Workplace Information Environment (WIE)

In Chapter 1 we presented Taylor's (1991) model of information use environments (IUE). This model explains the fluid, evolving, temporary and often messy context of information use. Yet the model also highlights tangible aspects and points of departure for dissecting the IUE. This book brings forth different perspectives on information use, from those focused on the actual activities to those concerned with the broader information culture at work. All these aspects highlight specific aspects of the IUE. The complexity of information processes and the increasingly central value of information itself in work calls for an understanding of workplace information from a holistic and integrative perspective.

We regard Taylor's model as remaining highly relevant for understanding the role of information at work. The model is grounded in opposing the assumption 'that we can describe information behaviour by starting with the system, the service, the knowledge base, or the information carrier'. Rather, Taylor proposes: 'To use these as definers of useful information is misleading: only the recipient, the user, can define information in his or her context' (Taylor, 1991, 250). Another foundation in the model is the identification of the keystones of the context for workplace information and the focus on information use in these contexts. Taylor focuses – and explicitly states so – on groups, not individuals. This can be seen as an early attempt at practice-oriented approaches within information studies by emphasising socially shared understandings as the basis for interactions in the context of work.

Below, we present the WIE model. This builds on Taylor's work but updates it to the current needs for studying information at work. We have identified the weaknesses of Taylor's original model and strive to address them in our model. We have recognised some of the key developments in the current workplace, for instance the impact of new technology, and included the implications of these developments in the model.

We begin by presenting a more complex view of the core concepts in Taylor's model, namely information and information use. We move on to show an expanded view of IUEs, acknowledging the existence of several intertwined IUEs within and beyond the workplace.

Information and information use

Taylor (1991) notes, with reference to King (1982), that information to be used may be in the form of raw data or interpreted information. Toms, in Chapter 2, is in the same line in her discussion between data, metadata, information and knowledge. She argues that most of the information used at work is already to some degree processed. Information use is the key foundation of Taylor's model. Taylor himself, in the concluding section of his article, pondered on the addition of *information* as a keystone of its own. We very much agree with this proposal. In line with Taylor (1991) and Wenger-Trayner and Wenger-Trayner (2014, 13) we see information and knowledge or the body of knowledge of any profession being only partially recordable, and that information and knowledge is intertwined with people's continuous engagement within their practice, where information is applied and reconstructed as it is used. Second, we see an inclusion of both verbal and non-verbal formats of information as an obvious aspect of workplace information. However, we do not think that separating information to form its own category is the best way to incorporate information within a new WIE model, but rather that the informational perspective permeates all keystones in the model.

There is, however, also a need to problematise the concept of *use*. Kari (2007) regards *use* as the practical impact of information, as separate from information *effect*, indicating that information may impact us emotionally and influence us even when we did not actively seek it. In times of social media flows and constant mobile interaction where information, including work information, is constantly pushed at us, the effect-aspect of information becomes more evident. Encountering such 'unexpected' information may lead to innovation and discovery, or simply information overload and distractions. This again suggests an emotional effect of information, where updates may alter opinions or demotivate workers. This changes the premises for determining relevance of information and complexity of information itself, as discussed by Pennington and Ruthven in Chapter 6.

Information is not the only thing that can create effect, however. In Chapter 5, Byström and Pharo discuss the agency of information artefacts, and suggest that no information artefact is a neutral intermediator of information. Information artefacts have agency of their own and, in a sense, exercise power over what information is highlighted as relevant and 'useful' for different work. Widén and Steinerová in Chapter 3 take a similar stand by indicating that information culture provides a backdrop for which information is value and shared information. In Chapter 4 Macevičiūtė and Thivant point out that for effective information use in an organization, effective information management is a key. If relevant information is not acquired, organized, retrieved and disseminated, this may lead to erroneous decision making and information problems in the organization. Information use in a workplace, therefore, is not something that happens spontaneously; instead it is a result of much groundwork, within often almost invisible processes in the organization, which workers may take for granted.

Expansion of the IUEs towards workplaces

A workplace consists of sets of people and most large organizations will contain multiple professional groupings specialising in areas such as finance, human resources, health and safety and legal matters alongside the main area(s) of their business. Taylor (1991) specifically addressed doctors, engineers and legislators as three separate professions with their separate, specific IUEs. Even if there is an implicit understanding that IUEs do not exist in isolation, the relationships between IUEs are not considered in Taylor's work. However, an organization may have all these professionals and/or representatives of several other professions or occupations among their employees, all with their own IUEs. From a technological perspective, various professions also need various forms of technology, some more advanced, others more fine-grained, for example. This also makes it complicated to develop technology, particularly if we wish it to cater for several groups.

Our main adjustment to Taylor's model thereby concerns the acknowledgement of parallel, heterogeneous professional/occupational groups that interact in a workplace. Wenger-Trayner and Wenger-Trayner (2014, 13) note that '[f]or professional occupations, however, the social body of knowledge is not a single community of practice' but formed as a landscape of practice 'consisting of a complex system of communities of practice and the boundaries between them'. In Taylor's terminology, a workplace consists of several IUEs that share some aspects, but differ in others, and more importantly must relate to each other. Turning back to Wenger-Trayners:

> All these practices have their own histories, domains, and regimes of competence. The composition of such a landscape is dynamic as communities arise and disappear, evolve, merge, split, compete with or complement each other, ignore or engage the other. Landscapes of practice are coming into focus as globalisation, travel, and new technologies expand our horizons and open up potential connections to various locations in the landscape.   (Wenger-Trayner and Wenger-Trayner, 2014, 15)

This means that information, information objects and information artefacts cross boundaries between several IUEs, coloured with possibly different cultural and managerial approaches to information. This creates dynamics as to value of information and granularity of information required. Whereas in one IUE a general idea in the form of compiled, overall description is sufficient, a more detailed picture with specified calculations about the same matter may be required in another IUE. Thus, in studying a workplace, several IUEs that work in parallel need to be accounted for. Increasingly, accomplishment of work tasks requires expertise from several professions. As the solution unfolds, several professions' IUEs are activated and actualised, including the professionals' views on the problems and their resolutions. Consider, for instance, surgery, where the surgeons' specialised information use intertwines with the nurses' and technological experts' in performing an operation. All these professions' IUEs are needed for a successful surgery. This leads us to conclude that the single-profession IUE that Taylor presents provides only a limited view of the actual complexity of information use at the workplace.

Expansion of the IUE beyond workplaces

Taylor (1991) focused specifically on work-related IUEs. He acknowledges how informational aspects of professionals' core work tasks traverse the boundaries of a single workplace. Workplaces are not islands, however. We see a need to expand Taylor's view to acknowledge how work IUEs are interwoven with IUEs outside work. In a time of ever more entwined work and leisure enabled by internet technology, work is not enacted separately from other contexts of everyday life. This suggests that the merging of various professional IUEs with ones for other contexts becomes necessary to accommodate situations where information is sought and found from sources in people's larger life-world instead of solely professionally legitimated sources. One example is using the public internet to find out how to use an information system or information tool, such as the newest version of a word processing program, and solving the problem by reading about others' experiences or solutions on a discussion forum or watching a video over the internet rather than using the company's IT support.

Expansion towards trajectory of time

Workplaces, furthermore, are not constant. Taylor (1991) did not explicitly address the effect of time on IUEs. We consider this as another major adjustment of the original model. Whereas professions and occupations have traditionally been seen as relatively constant, particularly in defining their core activities, there have always been changes in different aspects of work. New knowledge and new technology are two examples of areas that can have a profound impact on how work is carried out and organized in workplaces. In particular, information technology is currently a driver of many changes in workplaces, both by providing access to a vast amount of any type of information and by facilitating work from a distance. Changes may, moreover, vary across professions, with some changing fast and profoundly, while others evolve at a slower pace. Even in the same organization, some groups' IUEs may change faster or more often than others'. This also manifests in more lack of control and uncertainty for some people in the organization as compared to others. This uneven pace, and at times unexpected developments, may in turn create tension. For some, changes may be welcome, even offering a new exciting work path, while for others they may feel threatening and stressful.

The keystone aspects

Sets of people in the workplace

Practice-theoretical approaches to workplaces often emphasise that established routines and ways of handling information create unspoken and subtle expertise that newcomers learn as part of participating in work activities with more experienced peers, who already have developed 'a way of knowing', a kind of tacit understanding of codified, embodied and social cues in their context (Lloyd, 2006). As Widén and Steinerová point out in Chapter 3, each employee enters the workplace with his or her own information preferences and patterns based on their personalities and earlier experiences. At the workplace, however, it becomes necessary to adapt to the routines of that particular workplace influenced by their information culture. Both the information practices and the information culture may be explicit but more often they reflect tacit elements in the form of norms and traditions that govern the workflow. To work effectively it is therefore necessary to adjust personal preferences to the prevailing routines. An information culture as well as information practices, however, are evolving and influenced by workers. Newcomers to a workplace bring with them new knowledge and new skills, which may, depending of the information culture, contest and ultimately change the information practices in the workplace (e.g. Nordsteien and Byström, 2018). Without denying the social nature of an individual, Byström and Pharo in Chapter 5 argue that personal characteristics nuance how the workplace practices play out in activities leading to information use. Wenger-Trayners see, like many practice theorists, that competence is legitimated in the practice, but that it:

> is not static, however. It shapes personal experience but can also be shaped by it. It is both a stable and shifting as it lies in the dynamic between individuals' experience of it and the community's definition of it. Indeed, competence and experience are not a mere mirror-image of each other. They are in dynamic interplay. Members of a community have their own experience of practice, which may reflect, ignore, or challenge the community's current regime of competence. Learning in a community of practice is a claim to competence: it entails a process of alignment and realignment between competence and personal experience, which can go both ways. . . . Any new experience that does not quite fit the regime of

competence may cause the community to inspect and renegotiate its definition of competence. Or not.

(Wenger-Trayner and Wenger-Trayner, 2014, 14)

In defining information artefacts in Chapter 5, Byström and Pharo refer to socially and culturally constructed knowledge, or a 'regime of competence', that is communicated by people. They claim that in this intermediary process, a person becomes an information source and thus an information artefact herself; either in her capacity of delivering expertise (e.g. in a role of a doctor) or in her capacity of delivering signs to be interpreted through such expertise (e.g. in a role of a patient). This indicates that there are several sets of people a workplace who interact and bring into interactions knowledge and expertise of various types, and that for a workplace even people who not are employed there can provide useful information.

Macevičiūtė and Thivant in Chapter 4 present the importance of personal information management, the employee's own activities to manage tools and information content in the information flow. Each employee continuously receives information, for instance in the form of reports, instructional guides, messages or e-mails. For effective work performance these need to be managed by the employee. Taylor (1991, 250) stresses that information use may be both rational and irrational, but that what seems to be irrational at first sight may in fact be part of an employee's personal information management style and reduce the employee's information overload. Personal information management may also be a reason why people act against norms and traditions (Huvila, 2013), as well as explain variation and discrepancies in handling information. Workplaces are also arenas for human elements such as personality, personal habits and emotional reactions (Furnham, 1994; Muchinsky, 2000), and increasingly so as leisure and work blend. Technologies provide constant access and availability that can be a source of stress (Barley, Meyerson and Grodal, 2011), but flexibility, freedom, saves money and time on commuting and might as a result increase employee wellbeing (Gajendran and Harrison, 2007). Nevertheless, the personal information management becomes an important aspect of work.

Work tasks and duties

Taylor's IUE model occasionally makes reference to workplaces but more often operates in the level of professions/occupations. To increase the model's applicability as a conceptual framework for studies on workplace information, we orientate it towards workplaces and work tasks as the main unit of performing work. In Chapter 2, Toms refers to a standard definition of work as 'activity involving mental or physical effort done in order to achieve a result' that often is understood as 'task or tasks to be undertaken' (*Oxford English Dictionary*, n.d.). She furthermore notes that most work today involves tasks that 'create, manipulate, interpret and use information'. This leads her to propose that work is dependent on data and information that create information flows, on information processes that 'act on' data and information as well as interactive activities that connect people and objects. This means that information work can be studied with focus on activities and tasks that are part of the workplace as an ecosystem.

In Chapter 5, Byström and Pharo exemplify the use of information artefacts by relating them to information-related activities of information need, seeking and searching. They suggest that these activities and information artefacts have multiple relationships. Information needs are a result of expectations, values and traditions of the context, rather than something solely connected to a present situation or a work task (or the person attending to it). Part of this context is formed by the available information artefacts, which also create expectations to, as well as constrain what kind of 'answers' are available and preferred, and how difficult or costly the 'answers' will be.

These themes are also uncovered in complementary discussions in other chapters. In Chapter 4, for example, Macevičiūtė and Thivant show how management structures and systems arise to facilitate our work tasks. These solidify existing practices in such a way that we can create a shared vocabulary of tasks, processes, activities and artefacts which allow for shared understandings, differentiation from other organizations and the creation of corporate strategy. In short, they allow people within organizations to answer the question 'How do we do things here?' However, they risk ossification of processes, with the result that processes cannot change or improve because 'that's not how we do things here'.

In Chapter 6, Pennington and Ruthven show how the information objects we use to do our work have properties that can be used to differentiate each other and their value or potential for work. They discuss how the same criteria may be used in radically different settings, e.g. we all want high-quality information for our work, but how we assess quality, novelty or reliability may differ in work settings. Just as some information artefacts have taken on particular forms over the years to fit with certain tasks (menus, instruction manuals, newspaper articles, etc.), other artefacts are evolving in form to fit with new tasks or tasks that are themselves changing. A rich area for workplace information is then in this space of change where our tasks are changing at the same time as the artefacts we use to complete the tasks are also changing.

Settings within the workplace

Today work that is undertaken by on-demand workers and in temporary teams is becoming increasingly common alongside traditional, occupation- or profession-bound employment. This means that the relevance of professions and long-term contracts is diminishing, and that projects conducted by time-limited teams are becoming a more common way of organizing a workforce. Such team-based views on work differ when compared with traditional department-based views by placing short-term goals at the forefront, creating altered requirements for information cultures and information management. Moreover, work carried out by temporarily assembled teams emphasises different aspects of information artefacts and information attributes to facilitate collaboration. Information processes are ever more collaborative, increasing the importance of interactive information retrieval and collaboration in information creation and use (Shah, 2014). Technology permits new working practices with cloud services allowing teamwork across time zones and virtual reality applications creating realistic spaces for business meetings (Colbert, Yee and George, 2016). Collaborating across company borders and networking across work contexts may at times be more important than connecting to the next-door colleagues. Global multilingual companies create new challenges for information sharing with colleagues (Ahmad, 2018). Diversity and its implications for teams and hence information culture, management, artefacts and attributes will need further investigations.

In Chapter 3, Widén and Steinerová underline how the concept of IUE highlights the complexity of information processes where different entities constantly and evolvingly interact. They notice that Taylor's IUEs focus on mostly on concrete entities, such as 'the actual information landscape, the tools, objects, and actors', whereas values, attitudes and traditions at the workplace are less focused upon. Placing more emphasis on the information culture model enriches our understanding of workplace information environments by illuminating how values and traditions shape workplaces, as for instance by providing and constraining information access. As underlined by Widén and Steinerová, the pervasive effects of information culture on workplace information use make it central to our understanding of workplace information environments.

Byström and Pharo take a practice-oriented approach to a workplace as a setting. Most activities in the workplace, including use of information and information artefacts as well as their associated strategies and goals, relate to formal and informal social norms and conventions of the workplace (cf. Salancik and Pfeffer, 1978; Giddens, 1984). In due course, the most regular information is made readily available in order to make work flow efficiently, and as a consequence some knowledge gets prioritised. Furthermore, they become part of the activities learned in relation to general and local work practices (e.g. Taylor, 1991; Wenger-Trayner and Wenger-Trayner, 2014). All participants, as well as the material and intellectual objects of the practice, including information artefacts, carry with them traditions, values, expectations and an agreed-upon set of facts that form the specific work context. In addition to rules and norms that regulate and guide the activities in a workplace, there are a number of information tools that affect what kind of working is possible.

Organizations of today are challenged in controlling and managing information flows. Telecommuting has developed fluid organizational structures where communication is rather peer-to-peer and task-based than management-ruled. Security risks are increasing as workers might work on insecure networks outside an employer's control. Control over data, information and information flows is changing. Cloud computing suggests open questions on who controls data and for what purpose information may be collected. Byström and Pharo discuss how tools for collaboration are increasingly merging with tools for storage and how cloud storage makes the data accessible from anywhere, which dramatically changes the possibilities for working outside the traditional physical workplace. At the same time, this creates challenges for secure and ethical handling of information (cf. Lindh and Nolin, 2016). Rapid technological development requires also change management. For instance, communication technology allows the tracking of employee activities and performance, prompting new ethical and managerial challenges.

Openness to innovation and technology may in times of rapid change provide an important business edge. At the same time, organizations also need to consider the added value of technology in itself. In Chapter 4, Macevičiūtė and Thivant explain the concept of information management. Information management concerns the management of information content, processes and tools for effective information use, both from a perspective of reaching organizational goals but also considering the employee as implementing processes and tools. Thivant and Macevičiūtė point out, in line with Taylor (1991), that it is humans who decide the usefulness of information systems. Technology lacks value in itself and needs to be curated for the employees. New information tools and processes such as artificial intelligence, social media and tools we may not yet even foresee put pressure on effective information management of and with these tools. Artificial intelligence may, however, also develop forms of automatic information management supporting the managerial process.

Resolutions in the workplace

Taylor's final keystone was on resolutions: that is, what is perceived as potential solutions to work problems. Our reorientation of Taylor's work problems to workplaces and work tasks calls for a reorientation of resolutions as well. What do we use for work tasks and from where do solutions to work tasks come?

A traditional view is that resolutions are information and information sources. In Chapter 5, Byström and Pharo take an advanced position and define information artefacts as means that mediate information work and means for resolution within workplace environments. They identify several conceptualisations that information artefacts are granted in workplace information studies. Information artefacts can be sources and channels of information, the first being an intermediator of information or knowledge sought for and the second providing access to the information source. Information channels have been seen either as means to allow communication (e.g. a mobile phone or virtual meeting room) or as means to find a source (e.g. a colleague or enterprise search engine to locate project documentation). Information tools and information systems, including enterprise social media and intranets, are addressed as more general terms capturing multiple informational activities. Each information artefact can furthermore be described by a number of scalable features that have an effect on how information-related activities, such as information needs, searching and seeking, play out in performing work. For instance, an information artefact can be, to differing degrees, persistent or formal; can be used for several purposes, even other than informational ones; can be digital or physical, static or constantly revised, etc. Examples that Byström and Pharo provide of information artefacts are tools that support core information practices at the workplace, such as searching for and seeking information, information sharing and collaboration from the perspectives of workers; and from the perspective of workplaces, that is taking a more managerial view, tools for governing, systematising and managing information. This highlights that information artefacts both provide access to information for the workers and also keep track of the tasks and processes. In other words, they harmonise the content and co-ordinate the temporal diversity among participating professionals' work tasks.

Their broad definition acknowledges both material and non-material formats as well as including entities that are not originally created as information artefacts, but have been used for informational purposes. Essential to their definition is that any entity that is used for mediating knowledge can be viewed as an information artefact. This has powerful implications for how we see resolutions within workplaces as human agency can reconfigure and reconstruct information artefacts in practice. This means that information artefacts are not primarily or only static, storable and findable information objects, but entities that evolve over time, affecting and being affected by the context of their use. Thus, both a record in an organizational archive *and* a colleague in the next-door office may both be considered as information artefacts, the former more constantly so (although it may be used in different ways and for different purposes over time), the latter in certain situations (for example, when they are turned to in their capacity of an expert). This makes information artefacts plastic, flexible to changes in their context and gaining purpose through their use.

The space of resolutions is rapidly changing also through new functions for technology in workplaces. The role of artificial intelligence in communicating information is already evident in automated translation, chat services and data-driven narratives. Analysing information quality may, therefore, move onto programming of algorithms that pick up e.g. fake news or translation errors. Increasingly machine learning may develop competencies to create more reliable information than human intelligence that may be biased, subjective or driven by an agenda. Equally, such techniques may have their own biases and agendas that are far more difficult to spot. How information that is automatically created changes the way we employ concepts such as cognitive authority could result in profound changes to our work information environments. Machine learning is also overtaking analytical information tasks such as classification and tagging and becoming the default solution for such tasks. Therefore, our default assumptions about which resolutions are human mediated and which are machine mediated are shifting rapidly.

As described in Chapter 6, the highest level of relevance from Saracevic's classification was motivational relevance, which incorporates notions of the user's goals and preferences. Already we are seeing in areas such as proactive information delivery (Holz et al., 2005; Vuong, Jacucci and Ruotsalo, 2017) systems that are moving towards detecting information needs before a user is consciously aware of the needs. Therefore, we are moving towards resolutions being offered without us having to ask for them. Such systems may also take into account our preferences for form, source and other attributes of information. The extent to which we can develop machine learning algorithms that also cater for analytics of less tangible forms of information such as pictures and communication tone, for instance irony, remains to be seen but again there seems a shift to machines not simply supporting resolutions but creating these resolutions for human choice.

Information is increasingly mediated through new formats such as images, short messages in tweets and tags. Increasingly, many employers are encouraging employees to be both consumers and creators of 'social' information whilst other employers create strict rules about social media use to retain their brand image. How to create good information cultures whilst retaining management over information in such a fluid information space is pre-occupying many corporate minds.

New workplace environments will nearly always mean using new tools each of which have their own affordances and offer different (parts of) resolutions; sometimes these tools are only available in that workplace, sometimes they are a choice from a range of similar-ish alternatives. Using modern communication tools is becoming a key workplace literacy. With so many tools available, and our understanding of how to best use them only gradually emerging, our literacy has to start with asking what tools are available before asking how best to use them to achieve resolutions. As tools change and become obsolete, so may our repertoire of resolutions force us to create new ones.

Workplace Information Environments

From the discussion above, we present our modified version of Taylor's IUE in Figure 7.1. The Workplace Information Environment (WIE) needs to be considered as a complex environment where information comes in various formats and with a variety of uses. The WIE consists of several intertwined IUEs which represent the professionals at the workplace or the work tasks and their requirements. The WIE moreover expands

1. Sets of people in the workplace	2. Work tasks and duties

• Professions and occupations
  – Defined by formal standards and education
  – Defined by divisions/teams
• Personal information management
• Individual characteristics
  – Demographic variables
  – Attitudes/experiences
  – Individual differences
  – Irrationality, emotions
• Workplace information literacy
	• Continuously evolving (within task and between tasks)
	• Single IUE: Each involved IUE has discrete classes of tasks and duties
	• Multi IUE: Involved IUEs create/adjust/interact with shared classes of tasks and duties
	• Problem dimensions (e.g.)
	  – Well structured/ill structured
	  – Complex/simple
	  – Assumptions agreed upon/not agreed upon
	  – Familiar/new patterns
	  – Task categorisations

3. Settings	4. Resolutions in the workplace

• Organizational structure
• Domain of interest
• Change over time
• Information culture
• Collaboration
• Information management
	• Data, Information and Knowledge
	• Textual, Social, Corporeal
	• Information artefacts:
	  information sources, channels, tools, systems and objects
	• Information attributes:
	  relevance, metrics, object properties
	• Information uses:
	  enlightenment, problem understanding, instrumental, factual, conformational, projective, motivational, personal or political
	• Information-trait continuums:
	  quantitative, data, temporal, solution, focus, specificity of use, aggregation, causal/diagnostic continuum

Figure 7.1 *Workplace Information Environment (WIE); a modification of Taylor's IUE (1991)*

beyond the workplace, including also the activation of out-of-work IUEs to complete work tasks.

Adding in the concept of time, we arrive at the representation of Workplace Information Environment (WIE) shown in Figure 7.2, where the four components of the WIE are presented as developing over time. This implies that any WIE is a dynamic entity, typically coming from previous WIEs but also heading towards new WIEs.

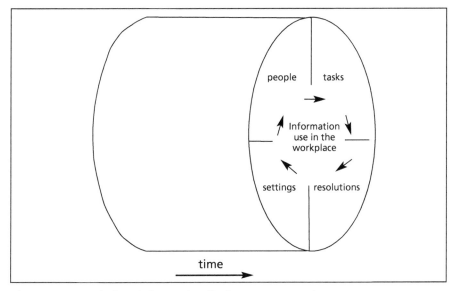

Figure 7.2 *Workplace Information Environment over time*

Future directions for workplace information research

As suggested in the first chapter, work and workplace information have changed radically in recent years, not least due to changes in the technology that supports our work. In this section we conclude with some thoughts on useful topics for future research in this area, inspired by the WIE model described above and by the chapters contributed to this book.

Our integrated view on WIE helps us see the different perspectives one may take in the study of workplace information. It illuminates how a particular perspective may shed in-depth light, while a more holistic view in turn may reveal wider connections. Depending on which of these perspectives one chooses for studying information use at work, a particular aspect is explored. Traditionally these perspectives also result in particular research methods. In this book the chapter authors call for the use of non-traditional methods and breaking boundaries. A productive, even if demanding and complex, research agenda for moving research on workplace information forward would be a combination of these different perspectives, both by combining theoretical perspectives and methodology. By focusing on e.g. a certain activity within complex decision-making tasks, one could study how information artefacts and attributes play out in the process of information use, relating these aspects to information culture and information management in the organization. On the other hand, already by being aware of the other perspectives and aspects that play out on WIEs, even the more focused research designs may be better informed about their delimitations, which increases the quality and comparability of research in the area.

If we take Ann, our cardiologist, as an example, one could explore a challenging task where a patient has been wrongly diagnosed. Will the information sources that led to the wrong diagnosis lose legitimacy, or does she find her information need insufficient, or is there a new discovery embedded in the problematic diagnosis? Why did the information artefacts provide her no warning about possible wrong diagnosis? To which information source will she turn for information this time, and for what reason? How much attention will she pay to the reliability of the information she finds, does she seek additional verifications? How is her choice of information source and her attention to information quality related to the information culture of her team and the hospital in which she works and the way information flow is managed therein? Studies like these would show how these various aspects of workplace information interact and might reveal unexpected patterns for further research.

We may also look at how Liila, our journalist, faced with an unexpected scoop will use information in the process of validating the information she has encountered. Will the fact that she is working for a newspaper with a traditional information culture deter her from publishing the scoop? Will the efficient management of digital information sources within her newspaper help her to identify more quickly the validity of what she has heard? Will she turn to alternative channels, and search for unvalidated reports online by competitors? How will all these factors play out in her ultimate decision to trust this scoop or to determine that it is based on rumours only? Turning to a more holistic research approach will help us understand her decision-making process more in depth.

Johan, our lawyer, has hired an assistant to help him manage the information he needs for his cases. Johan is independent minded and likes to trust his own instinct and experience. Will he challenge the information management system and the information culture at his law firm, when he unexpectedly runs into a case which confirms his independent thinking, contradicting that of information sources brought forth by his assistant and the opinions of his team? Will he challenge the information management system and the information culture at his law firm? His assistant emphasises that he has carefully identified key sources, the team is firm on their opposite decision. Johan, however, hesitates. What will he do and why? Will the source be decisive for his possible rebellion? Has the case been entrusted to him by an experienced colleague or is it something he runs into online? Will the complexity and richness of the information influence his thinking and provoke him to take an independent risk? How will the various aspects of workplace information interact as Johan ponders this step? How will the information culture, how information is managed, the information artefact that brought this information or the information attributes influence his decision? Probably a good explanation is to be found by exploring how these aspects interact. By only focusing on one aspect or conceptualisation, we can only understand one part of Johan's decision, while the decisive feature might have been another aspect or an interaction amongst two or more of them. We thereby suggest that future research directions would account for as many various aspects as possible, by employing a complementary array of methods.

As we noted above, extending IUE into workplaces requires us to acknowledge that individual IUEs will interact and studying these interactions can be a very fruitful area of study. Mary, whom we met in Chapter 1, is our regional manager whose agency deals with environmental problems and Bill, our coastal zone advisor, work for the same agency and therefore may be seen to have very similar IUEs. In one sense, their work is both environmentally focused, both roles require working with, aggregating and assessing multiple information sources and both, ultimately, make recommendations based on their information interpretations. Both may use very similar information and make their recommendations on similar professional knowledge. However, other aspects of their IUE may be very different. Mary has a much wider remit than Bill; she has more autonomy over her actions than Bill, whose work is very goal oriented. In addition, her work is more policy oriented, which brings in many considerations beyond the purely scientific. This can raise interesting questions about how they each deal with the same information and how different elements of their IUE influence their final decision making. We may ask, for example, about the degree to which Mary's policy agenda influences her recommendations versus the targeted instructions given by Bill's superiors. Or we may ask how the different information they are using leads them to similar or different decisions. Can we develop robust ways to compare IUEs, within and between workplaces, and the influence of their components that go beyond the purely anecdotal?

In order to further research on workplace information environments we, moreover, see the need for the following developments: up-to-date models for a changing work environment, a careful consideration of perspectives, conceptual clarity, considerations for the influence of new technology, technology-enabled research methods and working in tandem with artificial intelligence. We will argue for each in the following sections.

Models for a changed work environment

A first direction is how we can develop workplace information models that are more realistic in relation to the way people conduct their work in modern workplaces. Our journalist Liila was characterised as someone working in a fast-paced information environment which prioritises speed, both to gain and to disseminate information. Liila has to manage her own sources but also react to changing sources and deal with the almost instant feedback she receives on her own information creation. Johan's workplace information is not so frenetic but his information sources are more often digital, he deals more frequently with clients by e-mail than face to face and he has to learn about new sources of evidence (such as the data provided by new technology) to perform his duties. At one level, the 'work' of being a lawyer or journalist is the same as in previous generations but how the work is conducted and how the information environments change the way the work is done is radically different. A fruitful area of research may then be in considering what kind of models are suitable for explaining how such work is done and whether different models are necessary for different workplace situations.

Perspectives

As noted above, workplace information studies can take alternative perspectives on the same workplace phenomena that may lead to different conclusions about the phenomena being studied. If we study how people work, for example, what do we learn about working in comparison to focusing on certain work tasks and how they are performed? What does focusing on the role of technology in the workplace explain differently from focusing on the people using the technology? The way we pose our questions often leads to the choice of one perspective over others; however, a focus on one aspect of information workplace environment does not imply that other aspects are somehow out of focus or less interesting to answer. A focus on technology, for example, may not consider the human aspects of using that technology, whilst a focus on the individual worker may not consider wider issues of organizational efficiency and effectiveness. How, therefore, can we balance the need for specificity within workplace information studies, which argues for a narrower focus, against the desire to be able to compare and integrate studies, which argues for more holistic approaches?

Conceptual clarity

In many chapters we see discussions about conceptual clarity, or more often the lack of conceptual clarity, with different names being attached to what is effectively the same concept. Pennington and Ruthven in Chapter 6 conclude that the very central term in all workplace information studies, information itself, is hard to define, which consequently makes it a challenge to define the characteristics of information. This challenge is equally valid for the other information-dependent conceptualisations in the other chapters in this book. Sometimes the research literature shows an almost carefree indifference to defining important terms in such a way that they can be precisely studied, regardless of the perspective of study. One step forward may be in developing more formal vocabularies and categorisation schemas to compare studies and be able to investigate concepts across studies that use different theories and methods. As the chapters of this book have shown, this may be difficult due to different ways of viewing a workplace and the information-related activities taking place there. Thus, trying to force a single definition, for instance, on 'information' may delimit the phenomena to be studied, and be counterproductive to a holistic study of the phenomena of the workplace.

So rather than aiming for a single formal vocabulary, a 'thesaurus' of vocabularies from different perspectives bridging the perspectives could be a long-term goal for conceptual clarity. In order to work towards this, the value of clear definitions used in individual workplace information studies cannot be emphasised enough.

Influence of technology

As new technologies develop, the need for research on the impact and role of these technologies increases. New technologies may create whole new industries (social networks, e-commerce, etc.) or they may be simply complementary to existing modes of work. It is notoriously difficult to predict whether an individual technology will be a game-changer or simply another fad that increases the volume of work temporarily whilst nothing substantial changes in how we work. Nevertheless, technology studies will no doubt form a significant branch of workplace information research. The introduction of new technologies, such as virtual reality, will continue to raise questions about how to incorporate new affordances and potentials into workplace environments. New ways of creating data, from life-logging to wearable devices, also suggest interesting developments where organizations potentially may access personal data of employees. How this is best managed, and the ethical implications, however, are little understood.

As technology evolves so does also research methodology. In recent years we have seen a surge of research analysing big data, applying recording devices, on-the-go data collection through mobile technology, use of electrocardiogram, brain waves, skin conductance, etc. All these methods enable detection of patterns across a wide population, revealing large-scale trends that remained hidden before the evolution of data collection. Physiological measures enable a more concrete understanding of the mind body interconnectedness. The flow of information itself is also more easily detected through automated data collection. All these innovations enable both a wider quantitative understanding of trends and a more in-depth understanding of the human element. The influence of bodily reactions in times of work stress may be a more powerful argument for management to intervene. Large-scale patterns of software use or reactions to Twitter feeds may result in more informed decision making. We may also detect surprising patterns by the employment of new research methodology resulting in innovation and discovery.

Working in tandem with artificial intelligence

Artificial intelligence (AI) as a particular form of technology is currently raising many questions, including the extent to which AI and increasingly advanced algorithms can replace human workers but also can mimic emotional and intuitive sources of information. Some of the chapters have identified specific areas of future study. Macevičiūtė and Thivant in Chapter 4 envision AI components to be used to increase the efficiency of connection management according to the workplace needs and organizational decision making by seamless transmission of information. Toms in Chapter 2 concludes that technology will increasingly cause redesign of work and deliberates on future allocation between human and robotic workers. The automation of information-related activities raises ethical questions in cases where robots will aid the human, and handle or partially handle much of this interaction. In the same line of reasoning, Byström and Pharo in Chapter 5 ponder changes that 'algorithmic expertise' may cause in workplaces. Pennington and Ruthven in Chapter 6 identify this very same issue in automatically defining information attributes, with the interference of human domain knowledge. Is there a limit beyond which AI cannot reach or can AI be programmed to pick up even more subtle signals than humans? The increasing role for AI in workplaces creates new demands for workplace information literacy and communication skills, at times facilitating information access, transfer and sharing when the human element of being e.g. distracted, tired or not able to decipher information disappears.

Individual and social change of working

The rapid and voluminous development of technology is likely to cause changes not only in the ways we work with the technology, but how we work in general. Macevičiūtė and Thivant in Chapter 4 make a point of including the new tools and methods in the fabric of organizational information structures as a future task for information management. Toms refers to automation in Chapter 2, as do Byström and Pharo in Chapter 5. Toms concludes in Chapter 2 that new technologies are now part of the fabric of the digital workplace which is shifting what we mean by work. Byström and Pharo refer to information artefacts that perform work tasks on behalf of people, which changes what work we do, but also the prerequisites for working itself. Widén and Steinerová view the changing informational circumstances as challenging for a common information culture, shared values and common information practices, and an area of future research. They also emphasise the question of how professional information literacy is developed in digital environments. For workplace information studies this opens new research avenues regarding the role of information. How will the information culture be formed for a digital workplace? What kinds of requirements does it set for information management? How can information artefacts facilitate or hinder the bridging between physical and digital workplaces? Does this alter how information attributes are considered? Many workplaces still rely heavily on the physical proximity of their workforce to co-ordinate and consolidate the work activity and relationships between peers. Such a socio-cultural tradition of 'going to work' is strong and changing this is a major adjustment for individual and social work environments. It will be a challenge to both employees and employers to find socially acceptable and individually rewarding alternative ways of working and building work communities.

Concluding words

Macevičiūtė and Thivant concluded Chapter 4 by stating 'It [information management] takes a managerial perspective that includes such aspects as ownership, costing and pricing of information resources, security, relevance to organizational goals, effectiveness of information use in decision making, reduction of equivocality, and reduction of stress in the workplace.' This wide-reaching power of good information management to improve our work and working lives lies at the very heart of this book and the research it encapsulates.

The increasing mechanisation of our work may provide some answers to important questions of 'who does what work?' and 'how is this work done?' However, technological solutions can only provide partial answers. Work is a central theme of human existence; it can be a place for experimentation, creativity, inspiration and achievement but also has the potential to be a place of dehumanised, dispirited endurance. The difference can come from the knowledge of how to craft good WIEs and this knowledge demands input from many areas of academic research and practice. This text promotes research into positive WIEs as a component of positive human existences.

References

Ahmad, F. (2018) Knowledge Sharing in a Non-native Language Context: challenges and strategies, *Journal of Information Science*, **44** (2), 248–64.

Barley, S. R., Meyerson, D. E. and Grodal, S. (2011) E-mail as a Source and Symbol of Stress, *Organization Science*, **22** (4), 887–906.

Colbert, A., Yee, N. and George, G. (2016) The Digital Workforce and the Workplace of the Future, *Academy of Management Journal*, 59 (3), 731–9.

Furnham, A. (1994) *Personality at Work: the role of individual differences in the workplace*, Psychology Press.

Gajendran, R. S. and Harrison, D. A. (2007) The Good, the Bad, and the Unknown about Telecommuting: meta-analysis of psychological mediators and individual consequences, *Journal of Applied Psychology*, **92** (6), 1524.

Giddens, A. (1984) *The Constitution of Society: outline of the theory of structuration*, University of California Press.

Holz, H., Maus, H., Bernardi, A. and Rostanin, O. (2005) From Lightweight, Proactive Information Delivery to Business Process-oriented Knowledge Management, *Journal of Universal Knowledge Management*, **0** (2), 101–27.

Huvila, I. (2013) Meta-Games in Information Work, *Information Research*, **18** (3), http://InformationR.net/ir/18-3/colis/paperC01.html.

Kari, J. (2007) Conceptualising the Personal Outcomes of Information, *Information Research*, **12** (2), http://InformationR.net/ir/12-2/paper292.html.

King, L. S. (1982) *Medical Thinking: a historical preface*, Princeton University Press.

Lloyd, A. (2006) Information Literacy Landscapes: an emerging picture, *Journal of Documentation*, **62** (5), 570–83, https://doi.org/10.1108/00220410610688723.

Muchinsky, P. M. (2000) Emotions in the Workplace: the neglect of organizational behaviour, *Journal of Organizational Behavior*, **21** (7), 801–5.

Nordsteien, A. and Byström, K. (2018) Transitions in Workplace Information Practices and Culture: the influence of newcomers on information use in healthcare, *Journal of Documentation*, **74** (4), 827–43.

Oxford English Dictionary (n.d.) Work, https://en.oxforddictionaries.com/definition/work.

Salancik, G. R. and Pfeffer, J. (1978) A Social Information Processing Approach to Job Attitudes and Task Design, *Administrative Science*

Quarterly, **23** (2), 224–53.

Shah, C. (2014) Collaborative Information Seeking, *Journal of the Association for Information Science and Technology*, **65** (2), 215–36.

Taylor, R. S. (1991) Information Use Environments. In Dervin, B. (ed.), *Progress in Communication Sciences*, vol. 10, Ablex, 217–55.

Vuong, T., Jacucci, G. and Ruotsalo, T. (2017) Proactive Information Retrieval via Screen Surveillance. In *Proceedings of the 40th International ACM SIGIR Conference on Research and Development in Information Retrieval* (SIGIR '17), ACM, 1313–16.

Wenger-Trayner, E. and Wenger-Trayner, B. (2014) Learning in a Landscape of Practice: a framework. In Wenger-Trayner, E., Fenton-O'Creevy, M., Hutchinson, S., Kubiak, C. and Wenger-Trayner, B. (eds), *Learning in Landscapes of Practice: boundaries, identity, and knowledgeability in practice-based learning*, Routledge, 27–44.

Index